LETTERS

TO THE

RT. REV. JOHN HUGHES,

ROMAN CATHOLIC BISHOP OF NEW YORK.

BY

"KIRWAN."

FIRST SERIES.

PHILADELPHIA:
PRESBYTERIAN BOARD OF PUBLICATION,

CONTENTS.

CONTENTS.

INTRODUCTORY NOTE.

The pages that follow were written in the form of letters to Bishop Hughes, that they might readily gain the attention of those for whose benefit they are designed. The writer is a gentleman who has never taken any part in the Romish controversy, but having been educated in the Church of Rome, by parents of that faith, and having remained in that communion until mature years and patient thought enabled him to judge for himself, he became calmly but decidedly convinced that he must leave it, and seek the religion of the Bible among Protestants.

In these pages, the result of his own experience and observation, he gives the reasons that compelled him to abandon the church of his fathers, and the reasons why he cannot return to her embrace. The letters are written with great courtesy, frankness and ability, with the sprightly humour of an Irishman to an Irishman, and with an eloquence and earnestness that often remind us of some of the most celebrated passages from the Irish bar. They were first published in the *New-York Observer*, and were thence widely copied into other papers. They have been extensively sought for by Catholics who are beginning to inquire after the truth, and by others who wish to put them into the hands of those who are willing to read.

The temper of the letters commends them to a candid perusal, and the clearness of the argument and illustration will carry conviction to the minds of those who have the independence to decide for themselves by the light of the Bible and common sense.

The letters were furnished to me under an injunction of secrecy as to the Author's name, and having been requested by many individuals and societies to give them to the public in a form for preservation and further circulation, it is proper to say that the writer's character is an abundant guarantee for the fidelity of all the matters of fact here stated, and that he is prepared to maintain them if they should ever be called in question.

SAMUEL I. PRIME.

KIRWAN'S LETTERS

TO THE

RIGHT REV. JOHN HUGHES,

BISHOP OF NEW YORK.

LETTER I.

MY DEAR SIR,—Although an entire stranger to you, I have felt for many years greatly interested in your history and doings; and for the following reasons:

You are the chief pastor of a very important portion of the Roman Catholic Church in this country; and your ecclesiastical position makes you emphatically a public man. If a bishop in Mexico or Missouri, like many mitred priests, you might live unknown to fame; but as the papal bishop of the Commercial Metropolis of the Western world, and of the most populous and wealthy diocese of your church in the United States, this could not be expected. Position, you know, has much to do with our public character.

But in addition to your position, which is one of high influence, you possess the requisite qualifications to fill it. This is confessed by your most ardent opponents. By your genius, learning, and eloquence—by your sleepless devotion to the duties of your calling, you have obtained a position in the very first rank of the ecclesiastics of your church.

Besides, at whatever odds, you have fought like a man with all your opponents. In controversies religious and political, you have not shunned the hall of debate, nor discussion through the press. You have taken your positions adroitly, and you have defended them with remarkable skill. And even when convinced of the utter fallacy of your positions and defences, I have yet sympathized with your manly firmness. It is in human nature to respect the man that with an earnest soul contends for what he esteems right. And I must confess that as to some things, when the public voice was against you, your course met with my approbation.

Besides, if public rumour is worthy of belief, you have forced yourself into your present position by the force of your talents and character, from a social position comparatively humble. To me this is not the least of the reasons why I have felt interested in your career. The *men* of our race have been what is commonly called, self-made men. The heroes in history have been nearly all such. It requires high attributes both of mind and soul to rise above the disadvantages of family and fortune; and to take precedence of those who would fain believe that birth and wealth give a patent-right to the high places of influence. Your past history, unless I misunderstand it, must have had a liberalizing influence upon you. You must look at things on a larger and wider scale, and through a clearer medium, than if you had been cradled in crimson, and educated in a convent. You know the distinction between prejudice and principle—between what is entitled to belief, and what we have been educated to believe—between what is truly reasonable, and what is only ecclesiastically so. And I therefore address myself to you with a confidence far stronger that what I shall say kindly and truly, will be kindly and truly weighed, than if I addressed myself to a priest from Maynooth or St. Omers, educated merely in the literature of legends and liturgies, and whose mind only possessed what was distilled into it from others. I shall address you not merely as a priest or bishop; but as a high-minded and well-educated gentleman.

Permit me to say that there is yet another reason why I have felt interested in your career. You were born in Ireland, that land of noble spirits and of warm hearts—that sweetest isle of the ocean. And so was I. We are natives of the same soil And although in principle, by education, and in all my feelings, thoroughly American, yet I take a great pride in the high achievements of native Irishmen. America has had its Montgomerys, its Clintons, its Emmetts, its Porters, from Ireland. Its sons have adorned the bar, the bench, the pulpit, the army, the navy, the legislatures, the Congress of these United States. That there are multitudes from Ireland who are no loss to their own country, nor any advantage to this, cannot be denied. The reasons for this I may examine hereafter. But yet we have many fine illustrations of Irish genius, character and valour, all along our history. And I have regarded yourself as one of them, so far forth as genius and force of character are concerned. And I have often pointed you out as an illustration of the high respectability which Irish character is capable of attaining when relieved from the burdens that oppress and debase it. Hence I have regarded as your eulogy the sneers of those who have addressed you as "John Hughes the Gardener." Such taunts come not from true men.

Having said so much in reference to you, permit me now to say a word in reference to myself. I have just stated that I was born in Ireland. I may say to you in addition, that I was born of Roman Catholic parents, and received my early education in the full faith of that church at whose altars you now serve with such distinguished ability. I was baptized by a priest—I was confirmed by a bishop—I often went to confession—I have worn my amulets,—and I have said my Pater Nosters and my Hail Marys, more times than I can now enumerate. When a youth none excelled me in my attention to Mass, nor in the performance of the penances enjoined by the Father confessor. And whatever were my occasional mental misgivings, I remained a true son of the church until I had nearly reached the years of manhood. Then, on as full an examination of the subject as I could give it, I came to the conclusion that I could not remain a Roman Catholic. I first became an infidel. Knowing nothing of religion but that which was taught me by parents and priests, and thinking that that was the sum of it, when that was rejected, infidelity became my only alternative. Subsequently, by the reading of the Bible, and by the grace of God, I was led to embrace the religion of the Gospel. That religion I have now for many years professed, and in connection with a Protestant church. Unlike many who have left your communion, I have never bitterly assailed it. I am utterly unknown in the list of the champions of Protestantism versus Popery. But yet some recent occurrences have induced me to break a long silence, and to state in a series of letters addressed to your Right Reverence, the reasons which induced me to leave the Roman Catholic Church, and which prevent me from returning to it. Of these letters, this is the first. I ask of you for them a kind and candid perusal.

With great respect, yours,

KIRWAN.

LETTER II.

Causes of early misgivings—Priestly miracles—Purgatory—Praying to saints.

MY DEAR SIR,—In my last letter I stated to you that I was born of Roman Catholic parents—that I was baptized and confimed in your communion—and that for many years I have been in connection with a Protestant church. I stated that, whatever were my occasional mental misgivings, I remained a true son of the church until I had nearly attained the years of manhood; and that, then, on as full an examination of the subject as I could give it, I came to the conclusion that I could not remain a Roman Catholic. Permit me in the present letter to state to you the causes of my early misgivings as to yours being a true church, and as to its holding the true faith.

You know very well the common belief among the Irish peasantry that Papal priests can work miracles. Whatever may be the teaching of the priests themselves upon the point, such is the belief of the people, a belief strongly encouraged by the conduct of their spiritual leaders. Hence in diseases, the people resort, not so much to the physician, as to the priest—they depend less upon the power of medicine than upon that of priestly charms. Although the son of intelligent parents, and educated from my youth for the mercantile profession, the miraculous power of the priest is yet associated with my earliest recollections of him. And, as you know full well, the belief that this power is possessed by their priests, is one of the leading causes why the Papal Irish bow with such entire and unmanly submission to them.

In my youth there were two things which greatly shook my faith in the possession of this power. There resided not far from my parental residence a priest, whose fame as a miracle-worker was known all over the county in which he resided. The road to his house (called in that country a bridle road) went by our door. I frequently saw, in the morning, individuals riding by, with a little keg resting before them on the saddle, or a jug hanging by the horse's side. I often asked who they were, and where they were going? I was told that they were going to Father C.'s to get some of their sick cured. I asked what was in the keg, or jug? I was told that it was Irish whiskey to pay the priest for his cures. I asked why they went so early in the morning? I was answered that unless they went early they would not find him sober.

In one of the large interior towns of Ireland where I resided, the bishop of the diocese met his priests, or a part of them, once a year. This meeting was always held in the house where I resided, and over the store in which I was then a clerk. Among the priests that always met the Bishop was a Father B., whose fame as a miracle-worker was extensive. He had also a reputation for learning and eloquence;

2

and because of his connection with an old and wealthy family, exerted a wide social influence. He always staid with us when he came to town. About ten o'clock one night, after one of those meetings of bishop and priests, I went out to shut up the store windows; and hearing a singular noise in the gutter, I went forward, and assisted a man out of the mire. I soon recognized it to be Father B. the miracle worker. Running in, I announced with some excitement to the lady of the house that Father B. was drunk in the street. I received for my pains a stunning slap on the side of the face, with this admonition, "never say again that a priest is drunk." I staggered under the blow,—I assisted in cleaning off his Reverence. I gave him his brandy next morning. And young as I was, my faith in miracle-working priests was effectually shaken. Although fearing to draw the conclusion, I felt it, that God would not bestow miraculous power upon those who lived a life, not of occasional, but of habitual intemperance. And I would ask you, sir, whether all this pretension to miraculous power by your priests is not a gross imposition upon the people for the double purpose of keeping them in awe, and getting their money? Let the Bishop be silent, and the man of sense speak, and I have no fear as to the answer.

The doctrine of Purgatory, you know, sir, is one of the peculiar and most cherished doctrines of your church Indeed I do not know how your church could get along without it. My object now is not to reason with you about it, nor to controvert it; but to state to you a few facts in reference to it that made, in early life, a strong impression on my mind. You know that, in Ireland, the custom of the priest is, at a certain point in the service of the mass, to turn his back to the altar, and his face to the people, and to read a long list of the names of deceased persons whose souls are in purgatory, and to offer up a prayer for their deliverance from it. This is done, or used to be done, in the chapels on every Sabbath. To obtain the name of a deceased relative on that magic list, the priest must be paid so much a year, varying, I believe, with the ability of the friends to pay. If the yearly payment is not made when due, the name of the person is erased from the list. A circumstance arising out of this custom of your church, occurring in my boyhood, is distinctly before me. A respectable man in our parish died in mid-life, leaving a widow and a large family of children to mourn his loss. True to her religious principles, and to her generous instincts, the widow had her husband's name placed on that list, and heard, with pious gratitude, his name read over from Sabbath to Sabbath, with a prayer offered for the deliverance of his soul from purgatory. After the lapse of two or three years, on a certain Sabbath, the name of her husband was omitted from the list. The fact filled her with mingled joy and fear; joy thinking that her husband had escaped from purgatory: and fear, lest she had done something to offend the priest. On timid inquiry, she learned that his soul was yet in purgatory, but that she had forgotten to send in the yearly tax at the time it was due. The tax was promptly paid, and the name was restored on the next Sabbath. With this fact, sir, I am entirely conversant; for that widow was my own mother, who sought the release of the soul of my father from purgatory. Can you wonder, sir, that this incident made a deep impression upon my youthful mind, or that it shook my faith in your whole system? And, as far as memory serves me, Father M. was an amiable man, and above the ordinary level of the men of his calling.

Another fact which early impressed me in reference to purgatory was this. Your church makes a distinction between mortal and venial sinners. The former go to hell for ever—the latter go to purgatory, "whence they are taken by the prayers and alms offered for them, and principally by the holy sacrifice of the mass." Now I always saw that the *most mortal* sinners, that every body would say went to hell, could always have masses said for them as if they went to purgatory; provided their friends could pay; and that *less mortal* sinners, that people would say went to purgatory, were sent to hell, if their friends could not pay for masses for them. And their souls were kept in purgatory for a long while when their friends paid promptly every year; but their souls were soon prayed out whose friends could not pay long for them. Facts like these, sir, very early impressed my mind, and shook my faith in the religion of my parents and priests. And when, in maturer years, I could more fully consider them, they led me to reject religion as a fable cunningly devised by priests.

Again ; to pray to angels and saints is a doctrine of your church. I am quite familiar with your explanations of it; with the distinctions which your writers make to free it from idolatry. It is precisely the distinction which the heathen make to get rid of the same charge. Perhaps ere these letters are concluded I may return to this subject; I have only to do now with some of my early impressions in reference to it. In our parish chapel there were a great many pictures of saints. Whose pictures they were I do not remember. But on Sabbath morning, an hour before mass, I have often seen the poor people, and even some more wealthy and refined, going on their knees from the one picture to the other, and counting their beads, and bowing before them with external acts of the most profound and sincere worship. Although, then, I thought differently, I have not now a doubt but that it was idolatry. But the idea that struck me was this: here are some praying to Peter, or Paul, or John; the same pictures are hung up in ten thousand chapels all over the world, and in all these chapels persons are praying to them. Can these good saints hear but in one place, or can they hear all? If they can hear all, then they are omnipresent,—if omnipresent, they are gods. Thus we have as many gods as saints. But if they hear but in one place, then nine thousand nine hundred and ninety-nine out of the ten thousand are praying to an absent saint! This one thought, reverend sir, very early in life impressed my mind, and was not the least powerful among the causes which led me, eventually, to reject the authority of your church. More of these causes in my next.

With great respect, yours,

KIRWAN.

LETTER III.

Causes of early misgivings, continued—Confession—Holy wells—Prohibiting the Bible—An incident.

MY DEAR SIR,—In my last letter I commenced a statement to you of the causes which, in early life, caused my misgivings and distrust as to yours being a true church, and as to its holding the true faith. I referred to some incidents connected with the claims of your priests to miraculous power, with the doctrine of purgatory, and with praying to the saints. I shall now proceed with a statement of some more of those causes.

The doctrine of Confession is one of the primary doctrines of your church. It requires every good papist to confess his sins to a priest at least once a year. If any sins are concealed, none are forgiven. This doctrine makes the bosom of the priest the repository of all the sins of all the sinners of his parish, who make a conscience of Confession. And this is one of the sources of the fearful power which your priests have over your people. And with this doctrine of Confession, is connected the power of the Father Confessor to grant Absolution to the confessing penitent. It is sometimes affirmed, and then denied, to suit circumstances, that the priest claims such power. But Dr. Challoner in his "Catholic Christian Instructed," Chap. 9th, asserts this power, and on what he deems scriptural authority. And I never knew an individual who came from Confession, with the privilege of partaking of the Communion, who did not feel and believe that his sins were forgiven him. And if they were not immediately forgiven, they would be on the performance of the prescribed penances. You, sir, will not say, that I either misstate or misrepresent the doctrine.

Now for some of my early impressions upon this subject. Father M. held frequently his confessions at our house. He sat in a dark room up stairs with one or more candles on a table before him. Those going to Confession followed each other on their knees from the front door, through the hall, up the stairs, and to the door of the room. When one came out of the confessing-room another entered. My turn came—I entered the room, from which the light of day was excluded, and bowed myself before the priest. He made over me the sign of the cross, and after saying something in Latin, he ordered me to commence the detail of my sins. Such was my fright that my memory soon failed in bringing up past delinquencies. He would prompt me, and ask, did you do this thing, or that thing? I would answer yes, or no. And when I could say no more he would wave his hand over me and again utter some words in Latin, and dismiss me. Through this process I often went, and never without feeling that my sins were forgiven. Sins that burdened me before, were now disregarded. The load of guilt was gone. And I often felt, when prompted to sin, that I could commit it with impunity, as I could soon confess it and secure its pardon. And this, sir, is the fearful and fatal effect of your doctrine of Confession and Absolution upon millions of minds.

The questions however often came up—Why does the priest go into a dark room in the daytime Why not speak to me in English, and not in Latin? How can he forgive sin? What, if my sins, after all, are not forgiven? And I always found that I could play my pranks better after confession than before, for I could go at them with a lighter heart. Very early in life my confidence in this doctrine of Confession was shaken; and at a later period I came to the conclusion that it was a priestly device to ensnare the conscience, and to enslave men.

Another thing which made early a deep impression on my mind was this. On my first remembered journey to Dublin we passed by a place, called, unless I mistake, St. John's Well. It is, as you know, one of the "Holy Wells," of Ireland. There was a vast crowd of poor-looking and diseased people around it. Some were praying, some shouting; many were up in the trees which surrounded it. All these trees were laden, in all their branches, with shreds of cloth of every possible variety and colour. I inquired what all this meant. I was told: "This is St. John's Well, and these people come here to get cured." But what do those rags mean, hanging on the trees? I was told, that the people who were not immediately cured, tied a piece of their garments on some limb of the trees, to keep the good Saint of the Well in mind of their application. And judging from the number of pieces tied on the trees, I inferred that the number that went away cured were very few. I had previously read some travels in Africa describing some of the religious rites of the sable sons of that continent; and the thought that those performed around St. John's Well were just like them, occurred to me. I have no doubt but that the rites witnessed in my youth are performed there yet—that the rags of diseased persons are now streaming from those trees to remind the Saint of the requests of those who suspended them. There was always a priest present to hear confessions, and to receive the pennies of the poor pilgrims. And the impression then made upon my mind was, that it was a piece of paganism. And the rites and ceremonies about this Well, I learn, are nothing in comparison with those performed at the Wells of Saint Patrick in the County Down. I will here insert an account of a festival at St. Patrick's Well as given by an eye-witness.

"When or how the custom which I shall describe originated, I know not, nor is it necessary to inquire; but every midsummer eve thousands of Roman Catholics, many from distant parts of the country, resort to these celebrated holy wells to cleanse their souls from sin, and clear their mortal bodies of diseases. The influx of people of different ranks, for some nights before the one in which alone, during the whole year, these wells possess this power (for on all other days and nights in the year they rank not above common draw-wells), is prodigious: and their attendants, hordes of beggars, whose ragged garments, if once taken off, could not be put on again by the ingenuity of man, infest the streets and lanes, and choose their lodgings in the highways and hedges. Having been previously informed of the approach of this miraculous night, and having made ourselves acquainted with the locality of the wells, early in the evening we repaired to the spot: we had been told that we should see something quite new to us, and we met with what scarcely was credible on ocular evidence. The spot on which this scene of superstitious folly was exhibited, was admirably adapted to heighten every attendant circumstance of it; the wonderful wells, of which there are four, being situated in a square or patch of ground, surrounded by steep rocks, which reverberated every sound, and redoubled all the confusion. The coup d'œil of the square on our approach presented a floating mass of various coloured heads, and our ears were astonished with confused and mingled sounds of mirth and sorrow, of frantic, enthusiastic joy, and deep desponding ravings. On descending into the square we found ourselves immediately in the midst of innumerable groups of these fanatics, running in all directions, confusedly, in appearance, but methodically, as we afterwards found in reality; —the men and the women were barefooted, and the heads of all were bound round with handkerchiefs. Some were running in circles, some were kneeling in groups, some were singing in wild concert, some were jumping about like maniacs at the end of an old building, which, we were told, was the ruins of a chapel erected, with several adjacent buildings, in one miraculous midsummer's night by the tutelary saint of the wells, of whose talent as a mason they give, it must be confessed, no very exalted opinion. When we had somewhat recovered from the first surprise which the (to us) unaccountably fantastic actions of the crowd had given us, we endeavoured to trace the progress of some of these deluded votaries through all the mazes of their mystic penance. The first object of them all appeared to be the ascent of the steepest and most rugged part of the rock, up which both men and women crawled their painful way on their hands and bare knees. The men's clothes were all made so as to accommodate their knees with all the sharpness of the pointed rock; and the poor women, many of them young and beautiful, took incredible pains to prevent their petticoats from affording any defence against its torturing asperities. Covered with dust and perspiration, and blood, they at last reached the summit of the rock, where, in a rude sort of chair hewn out of the stone, sat an old man, probably one of their priesthood, who seemed to be the representative of St. Patrick, and the high-priest of this religious frenzy. In his hat each of the penitents deposited a half-penny, after which he turned them round a certain number of times, listened to the long catalogue of their offences, and dictated to them the penance they were to undergo or perform. Then they descended the rock by another path, but in the same manner and posture, equally careful to be cut by the flints, and to suffer as much as possible: this was, perhaps, more painful travelling than the ascent had been—the suffering knees were rubbed another way—every step threatened a tumble; and if any thing could have been lively there, the ridiculous attitudes of these descenders would have made us so. When they gained the foot of the hill they (most of them) bestowed a small donation of charity on some miserable groups of supplicants who were stationed there. One beggar, a cripple, sat on the ground, at one moment addressing the crowd behind him, and swearing that all the Protestants ought to be burnt out of the country, and, in the same breath, begging the penitents to give him one half-penny for the love of '*swate blessed Jasus.*' The penitents now returned to the use of their feet, and commenced a running sort of Irish jiggish walk round several cairns or heaps of stones erected at different spaces:

this lasted for some time. Suddenly they would prostrate themselves before the cairn and ejaculate some hasty prayers, as suddenly they would rise and resume their mill-horse circumrotation. Their eyes were fixed; their looks spoke anxiety, almost despair; and the operation of their faculties seemed totally suspended. They then proceeded to one end of the old chapel, and seemed to believe that there was a virtue, unknown to us heretics, in *one particular stone* of the building, which every one was careful to touch with the right hand; those who were tall did it easily; those who were less, left no mode of jumping unpractised to accomplish it. But the most remarkable, and doubtless the most efficient of the ceremonies, was reserved for the last; and surely nothing was ever devised by man which more forcibly evinced how low our nature can descend. Around the largest of the wells, which was in a building very much, to common eyes, like a stable, all those who had performed their penances were assembled, some dressing, some undressing, many *stark naked*. A certain number of them were admitted at a time into this holy well, and there men and women of every age bathed promiscuously without any covering. They undressed before bathing, and performed the whole business of the toilet afterwards in the open air, in the midst of the crowd, without appearing sensible of the observations of lookers-on, perfectly regardless of decency, perfectly dead to all natural sensations. This was a strange sight, but so nearly resembling the feast of lunatics, that even the voluptuary would have beheld it without any emotions but those of dejection. The penance having terminated in this marvellous ablution, the penitents then adjourned either to booths and tents to drink, or join their friends. The air then rang with musical monotonous singing, which became louder with every glass of whisky, finishing in frolicsome debauch, and laying, in all probability the foundation for future penances and more thorough ablutions. No pen can describe all the confusion, no description can give a just idea of the noise and disorder which filled this *hallowed* square, this theatre of fanaticism, this temple of superstition, of which the rites rival all that we are told of in the East. The minor parts of the spectacle were filled up with credulous mothers, half drowning their poor children to cure their sore eyes; with cripples who exhibited every thing that has yet been discovered in deformity, expecting to be washed straight, and to walk away nimble and comely.

"The experience of years had not shaken their faith; and though nobody was cured, nobody went away doubting. Shouting and howling and swearing and carousings filled up every pause, and 'threw o'er this spot of earth the air of hell.' I was never more shocked and struck with horror; and perceiving many of them intoxicated with religious fervour and all-potent whisky, and warming into violence before midnight, at which time the distraction was at its climax, I left this scene of human degradation in a state of mind not easily to be described. The whole road from the wells to the neighbouring town was crowded with such supplicants as preferred mortal half-pence to holy penance. The country around was illuminated with watch-fires; the demons of discord and fear were abroad in the air; the pursuits of the world, and the occupations of the peaceful, appeared put a stop to by the performance of ceremonies, disgraceful when applied to propitiate an all-compassionate Divinity, whom these religionists were determined and taught to consider jealous rather than merciful. I wish it were in my power, without insincerity, to pay a compliment to the Irish Catholic clergy. On this occasion they were the mad priests of these Bacchanalian orgies; the fomenters of fury; the setters-on to strife; the mischievous ministers of the debasement of their people, lending their aid to plunge their credulous congregations in ceremonious horrors."*

Now, sir, can you, as a man of high intelligence, regard these things in any other light than as the merest impostures to delude the ignorant? And what epithet sufficiently expressive of abhorrence can we apply to the priesthood who thus impose upon a credulous people?

I well remember yet another of these impostures. When a boy I often heard that on the morning of Easter Sunday, the sun might be seen dancing in the heavens and in the chapels, to express its joy on the anniversary of the resurrection of Christ. And I often wished to be where I could witness the phenomenon. It took place in a certain chapel, and in the presence of many pious and admiring beholders. An unbeliever in priestly miracles was present, who traced up the dancing of the sunbeams through the chapel to an individual managing concealed mirrors, so as to produce the wonderful effect! Of this I heard; and although it seemed incredible, yet it

* McGavin's Protestant, p. 403

made an impression on my mind. The probability of the imposture cannot be doubted by those who know that the earth which covers the grave of Father Sheely (who was convicted of treason, and hung in the County of Tipperary), when boiled in milk, cures a variety of diseases.

The Bible, with all its notes and glosses, as published by the authority of your own church, is denied by you to be a complete rule of faith. On this question I will not now enter, only so far as to say that this denial holds a very intimate connexion with its virtual withholding from the people. If not a complete rule, it may lead astray; and as it is capable of opposite interpretations, in some of its passages, the souls of the people must not be endangered by its general circulation. It is better to know nothing of the Bible, than in some particulars to misinterpret it! Your infallible church teaches both ways on a variety of subjects, and among the rest, on the circulation of the Bible. It allows it in Protestant countries, with some stringent regulations; it virtually forbids it in purely Papal countries. How many Bibles could your Reverence procure in Spain, Portugal, Naples, or Italy? How many Spaniards or Italians have ever read a Bible through? How many of the Irish peasantry that can read and write have ever read ten chapters of it? Now, sir, for years together I sat daily at table with a Catholic priest, who was a member of the family, and the curate of the parish; and I never saw a Bible used in the family. I never heard at table, or in the morning, or in the evening, a religious service. The numbers of the Douay Bible published by subscription in Folio, were taken in the family, but never read. And not only so, but I never heard a sermon preached in a Catholic chapel in Ireland; nor a word of explanation on a single Christian topic, doctrine, or duty. And before I was sixteen years of age I never read a chapter in the word of God, whilst in other respects my education was not neglected. I often asked the meaning of this thing and the other; but there was no explanation. Nor can one out of one thousand, in Papal countries, give a single reason for one of your peculiar doctrines or duties. And since in the maturity of my judgment I have examined this matter, I have greatly commended your wisdom in withholding the Bible from the people; if I were a bishop or a priest of your church I would do the same. I heard a man who lived near the Canada line, in Vermont, during the last war with Great Britain, tell the following story. "There was," said he, "much smuggling going on. Whenever we met a traveller with a pack of any kind, we ordered it to be searched. Honest men always said, 'search and welcome.' But whenever a man refused, or made any fuss about it, we always suspected that there were contraband goods in the pack; and we were never mistaken." You have brought contraband goods into the house of God, and the Bible tells the people so. Hence it is forbidden.

Light is the sure death of darkness. The circulation of the Bible will be the death of popery.

With great respect, yours,

KIRWAN.

LETTER IV.

Transition from Popery to Infidelity—Inquiry awakened—Abstinence from Meats—The Mass—Confession—Transubstantiation—Religion vanishes.

My dear Sir,—In my last two letters I have stated to you some of the causes of my early misgivings as to yours being a true church, and as to its holding the true faith. These causes I might multiply indefinitely; for you well know it to be a law of the human mind that when its confidence is once shaken, it sees causes of suspicion even in things true and honest. In my first letter I stated to you that when I deliberately rejected the authority and teachings of your church, I became an infidel. And my object in the present letter is to reveal to you the process through which my mind passed, in its transition from popery to infidelity. I believe that your Reverence will pronounce it a very natural one.

On reaching the years of maturity my mind was a perfect blank as to all religious instruction. And if such instruction is ever given by your church or priests, my advantages were peculiarly good for receiving it. Indeed I was even talked of as a candidate for Maynooth. Whilst my mind was filled with superstitious notions concerning meats and penances, and external observances, and legends, it was utterly ignorant of the Bible. With my Missal I was somewhat familiar: I said the Catechism when I was confirmed at the age of nine or ten; and that was the amount of my religious education. At the age of eighteen years the Catechism was forgotten, and the Missal was neglected; and as my conscience was uneducated, and my mind unfurnished with religious principles, the only test of truth left me was my common sense. I then became the associate of companions of Protestant education, who would sometimes ask me my reason for this and that observance; and not being able to give any, as none were ever given me, I was frequently put to the blush. I candidly state to you that it was in this way I was first led to bring to the test of my common sense, then my only standard, some of the doctrines and rites of your church. And this reveals the reason why your priesthood is so intensely concerned that Catholic children should be guarded from all contact with those of Protestant education. The spirit of inquiry is contagious; and pope, bishops, and priests fear it worse than the plague. Its indulgence, you know, either is, or leads to, mortal sin. Let me briefly state to you some of the effects of this spirit of inquiry upon me.

From my youth up I was taught to abstain from all meats on Fridays and Saturdays. Why on these days more than any other, I was never told. And if by mistake I was involved in the violation of this law, I felt a burden upon my conscience, of which confession could only relieve me. Circumstances led me to inquire into this matter. I saw good papists eating eggs, and fish, and getting drunk on these days; but this was no violation of the law of the Church! Yet if these persons should eat meat of any kind; or use gravy in any way, their consciences were troubled, and they must perform penance! This led me to ask, Is this reasonable? If I may eat meat on Thursday, why not on Friday? Can God, in things of this kind, make that to be a sin at one time which is not on another? I saw also persons, for whose moral worth I had the highest regard, eating meats on those days, and without any injury! And I came to the conclusion that your regulations upon this matter were unreasonable, and rejected them. And, as far as I now remember, this was my first step towards light and freedom.

Whether our course is upwards, towards the region of light, or downwards, towards that of darkness, one step always prepares for another. Devoted to reading at this period of my life, I perused, without discrimination, every thing that came in my way. Some book or tract, now forgotten, gave rise to some inquiries as to the Mass. I asked, What does it mean? I could not tell, though for years a regular attendant upon it. Why does the priest dress so? What book does he read from, when carried now to his right, and now to his left? What mean those candles burning at noonday? Why do I say prayers in Latin, which I understand not? Should I not know what I am saying when addressing my Maker? Why bow down, and strike my breast, when the little bell rings? What does it all mean? The darkness of Egypt rested upon these questions. I thus reasoned with myself; God is a spiritual and intelligent being, and he requires an intelligent worship. What worship I render him in the Mass, I know not. My intelligent worship only is acceptable to him, and is beneficial to me. I am a rational being, and I degrade my nature, and insult my Maker, by offering to Him a worship in which neither my reason, nor *His* intelligence is consulted. Having come to this conclusion, I gave up the Mass as a form of worship well enough fitted for an idol, but unfitted to be rendered by a rational being to the infinitely intelligent Jehovah. I have never been to Mass since, save out of curiosity to see how an ignorant people can be edified by what seems to me the most unmeaning and farcical of all the rites that ever man has devised. And you know, sir, that with all devotion and honesty a Catholic may wait on your Masses until his locks are as white as your surplice, and then pass into eternity without one single spiritual idea upon the subject of religion; resolving it all into external observances.

When I came to the above conclusion on the subject of the Mass, I experienced no great difficulty as to other matters which passed rapidly in review before me. Must I go to Confession? My prejudices said, Yes. My reason said, No. And my logic was simply as follows:—If I truly repent of my sins God will forgive me; if I do not, the priest cannot absolve me. And I spurned as unreasonable, and as an insult to my common sense, your terrible doctrine that "Every Christian is bound, *under pain of damnation*, to confess to a priest all his mortal sins, which after diligent examination he can possibly remember; yea even his most secret sins; his very thoughts; yea and all the circumstances of them which are of any moment." I ask you, sir, if this dogma of the Council of Trent is not a horrible dogma? It suspends upon confessing to a priest, what the Bible suspends on believing in Christ! Do you, sir, believe it? Can you believe it?

With yet greater abhorrence, I gave up the doctrine of Transubstantiation. As explained by Dr. Challoner, in his "Catholic Christian Instructed," Chap. 5, it means "that the bread and wine are changed by the consecration into the body and blood of Christ; and are so changed that Christ himself, true God, and true man, is truly, really, and substantially present, in the sacrament." With this doctrine in view, I went to witness the administration of the Eucharist, as you call it. I went to Saint Peter's in Barclay-street. The communicants drew around the altar upon their knees. With a little box in his hand the priest passed from one to the other, taking a wafer, smaller than that used in sealing a letter, from the box, and placing it upon the extended tongue of the communicant. I was always taught that the teeth must not touch the wafer;—that it must melt upon the tongue. This I find to be the law of your church. I witnessed the ceremony, as I had often done before. I retired from the scene, asking these questions: Is that little wafer the real body and blood of Christ? Does the priest, in that little box, not as large as a snuff-box, carry two or three hundred real bodies of Christ? Do these communicants, each in their turn, eat the real body and blood of Christ? My dear sir, I cannot express to you the violence with which my mind rejected the absurdity. Look at it in what light you may, it is abhorrent to our common reason—it gives the lie to every sense with which God has endowed us. It is a wicked imposition.

Having gone through this process, not with a light and trifling, but with a serious mind, my prejudices rising in stormy rebellion against my convictions, I raised up my eyes, and behold, my religion was gone! The priest was a juggler, and his religion a fable! Every thing that I had ever learned from parent and priest to esteem as religion, was now rejected as false; and not knowing but that this was all of religion that was in the world, I had no alternative but infidelity. I had no test of truth but my reason, and when I brought your system to that, I was compelled to reject it, not only as false, but as a monstrous absurdity, and with it, all religion.

Nor have I, dear sir, any hesitation in saying that the process of my own mind from popery to infidelity, is that through which multitudes of minds have passed, and are now passing. To an inquiring mind, which knows nothing of the Bible, infidelity is the fruit of popery. Hence in papal countries, whilst the masses are superstitious, the intelligent and educated are infidel. If they sustain the vulgar religion, it is for reasons of state. Hence, the infidelity of France, of Spain, of Italy. At the present hour the mind of these countries is more infidel than papal. And this is true of every country on the globe where your religion prevails. It makes the masses superstitious, and the intelligent, infidels.

And permit me to say, my dear sir, in reference to yourself, that I have far too high a regard for your intelligence to admit for a moment that you believe in the absurd doctrines which your church teaches. Like the ancient priests of Egypt, you must have one class of opinions for the people, and another for yourself. Will you say that this is harsh and uncharitable? None knows better than yourself that history affirms it of popes, cardinals, and bishops that have lived before you. On no other ground can I possibly account for your remaining an hour in the Roman Catholic Church.

With great respect, yours,

KIRWAN.

LETTER V.

Popery makes the masses superstitious, the intelligent infidels—Who go to confession?—Ireland—France—Other countries—Reasons why Popery debases—The days of Popery numbered.

MY DEAR SIR,—In my last letter, in which I stated to you the process of my mind in its transition from Popery to Infidelity, I asserted that the effect of your religion is, to make the masses superstitious, and the intelligent infidels, in all the countries where it predominates. Although the truth of this assertion is self-evident to the well-read mind, the briefest consideration will make its truth apparent to all.

How stands the matter in our own country? Who attend your Confessional, and your Masses in New-York? How many of the educated Irish, French, or Germans, ever whisper at your knees their sins, or ever bow at your altars to receive your wafers on their tongues, believing them to "be Jesus Christ himself, true God and true man," and believing that he is "truly, really and substantially present" in them? How many of these go to your churches? Let any body, wishing to know, stand at the door of

St. Peter's or St. Patrick's, on the Sabbath, and examine the multitudes who attend these places, and they will soon learn. And even when an intelligent person is seen mixing with those who attend on your masses, he goes merely through the force of habit, or to wait upon a female relative. Permit me to say that, with an acquaintance somewhat extended in our country, I know not a single layman, of any repute for learning or science, who believes in your distinguishing doctrines. There are some, I allow, of high standing and character who are nominally Catholics, but who, I learn on inquiry, are but nominally so. And the nominally Catholic is really an infidel.

And how stands the case as to Ireland, the land of our birth, where seven of her nine millions of people are Roman Catholics? Whilst its masses are with your church, is not its mind in opposition to it? And what has kept the mind of Ireland from being infidel, but the fact that the religion of the Bible stands out there with a greater or less degree of prominence in opposition to the religion of the priest? Thank God the Irish massacre did not exterminate Protestantism in the "fairest isle of the ocean."

And how stands the case in France, where your church, Nero-like, extinguished the lights of truth, and caused the blood of the Huguenots to run like water? Popery has managed France in its own way, without any let or hinderance, and what has been the result? It legislated God ou of existence—decreed religion to be a fable, and death to be an eternal sleep. Knowing nothing of religion but what it learned through the unmeaning rites of your church, and by the carnal policy of your priests, it sought to erase every trace of it from existence. And although France has recovered from the intoxication of the maddening bowl, and has risen to order from the wild chaos into which Popery plunged it, its mind is yet infidel. Voltaire is the pope of the mind of France, and Sue is the high priest of the people. Your dumb show of imposing ceremony is there esteemed, not as solemn, but farcical; and upon your rites but few attend save the peasantry and the women. And the world should hold the Papal church accountable for all the horrors of the French Revolution.

What is thus true of France is yet more true of the other Papal countries of Europe. If the nobility of Spain, Portugal, Austria, or Italy, are less infidel than in France, it is because they are less educated. Their masses are superstitious—their educated men, including many of their clergy, are infidels—and their men of fortune and spirit live without any moral restraint. Popery brings no strong moral influence to bear upon the mind and conscience of any people. In the proportion that its influence is strong, do people and nations sink in the intellectual, social, and moral scale.

That you yourself, dear sir, may see this, sit down

and candidly compare Connaught and Ulster, in Ireland. In the one, Popery almost exclusively prevails; in the other, Protestantism is in the ascendency. What a difference between them! Compare Ireland and Scotland—and although the land of St. Patrick is far richer than that of St. Andrew, yet how heaven-wide the difference between them! Compare Spain with England—Italy with Prussia—Rome with Edinburgh—Belfast with Cork: how wide the difference! Come across the Atlantic, and continue the comparison on our own Western continent. Compare Mexico to New England—Brazil to these United States—the city of Mexico to that of Boston, or New-York, or Cincinnati! How great the contrast! Come yet nearer home: compare the worshippers at St. Peter's in Barclay-street with those at St. Paul's in Broadway;—compare the attendants on your own ministry at St. Patrick's with those who worship God at the Brick Church, or at La Fayette Place, or at University Place. How wide the difference intellectually, socially, morally! And why is it that Papal countries and communities thus suffer, and so sadly suffer, when contrasted with other communities where there is an unshackled conscience and an open Bible? There must be some general law or cause in operation to produce results so uniform. What is that law or cause? Sir, it is the influence of that system of religion which you are seeking with so much zeal and ability to extend. The traveller in Europe need not be told when he crosses the lines that separate Papal from Protestant states; the obvious marks of higher civilization declare the transition with almost as much plainness as would a broad river or a chain of mountains. Popery, with infallible certainty, degrades man. Do you ask how? In this wise.

It takes from him the Bible, the revealed will of God, with all its clear light, with all its high motives to excite the soul to high and holy action; and without which neither civilization nor religion can be long maintained. Papal countries are countries without the Bible.

It withholds from the people all right moral instruction. It suppresses the preaching of the gospel, and substitutes for it the dumb show of the Mass. The Apostles turned the world upside down by preaching: but in Papal countries there is generally no preaching. I venture the assertion that there are multitudes of Catholic churches in Catholic countries where a sermon would be as great a rarity as would be the saying of mass in a Scottish kirk! And is it not one of the seven wonders of the day, that the present Pope, the pretended successor of that warm-hearted preacher, Peter, *has preached a sermon*, the first preached by a Pope in three hundred years!! Could Peter return to Rome, unless his long absence from the body has cooled his generous but impetuous spirit, I am afraid he would treat his pretended successors as roughly as he once did Malchus.

It withholds from the people the benign influences of Christianity, the great element in the development of civilization. It withholds the Bible;—the sermon;—it has instituted a worship which wants nothing of heathenism but the name;—that worship is performed in a language now unspoken by any living people;—it excludes all reading from the people but such as the priest permits;—acting on the principle that ignorance is the mother of devotion, it erects no schools for the instruction of the common mind;—it substitutes the feast day for the Sabbath,—the saints and the Virgin Mary for the Saviour;—confessions and penances, for faith in Christ;—and reverence for places, unmeaning rites, relics, for the fear of God. Sir, I say it with deep sorrow, Popery is not Christianity. It is a fearful perversion of the religion of God; and for the evidence of these assertions I again point you to its influence upon the people where there is nothing to counteract it. It has degraded the once noble Castilian until there is now none so mean as to do him reverence;—Italy, once the seat of empire, it has reduced to feebleness;—and the once chivalrous Italian, who carried the eagles of his country to the extremes of the world, to an ignoble slave. And it has rendered our noble-hearted, noble-minded, impulsive countrymen, the hewers of wood and the drawers of water in all the countries to which they emigrate. The degradation of Ireland, which has made it a byword, I charge upon Popery. If the priests of Ireland would give the quarter of what they receive for praying souls out of Purgatory, to the sustaining of common schools among the people, there might be three or more such schools sustained in every parish in that bleeding, famishing, yet noble country; and its sons would have an opportunity of rising to that position to which their native wit, eloquence, and genius entitle them.

These, sir, are, in brief, my reasons for asserting that the effect of your religion is to make the masses of your people superstitious. They have no intelligent views of God. They know nothing about the plan of salvation. Sacraments and ceremonies exert an undefined, mysterious influence. The priest exerts a ghostly, fearful power, before which the ignorant believer slavishly crouches, and of which he stands far more in awe than he does of the God who has made him.

And the very causes which render the masses superstitious, operate in an opposite direction upon the intelligent, and drive them into infidelity. They reason about your doctrines as the Earl of Mulgrave is said to have done with a priest who was sent to him by James II. of England, to convert him to Popery. "Sir," said he, "I have convinced myself by much reflection that God made man; but I can not believe that man can make God."

My dear sir, the days of Popery are numbered. The Bible is against it. Civilization is against it. The mind of the world is against it. Good people now pray for its downfall as earnestly as they do for that of Mahometanism. It may live through centuries yet to come ; but it will be as Judaism now lives ; or as Paganism lived in many dark corners of the Roman world long after its conversion to the Christian faith. But my own fear is that the Papal world, both as to its mind and its masses, will become suddenly infidel, as in France, and then pour down its legions upon the church of God, to blot it out of existence. The Romish church is one of the "gates of hell" which has poured forth armies of the aliens in opposition to the church of Christ ; but it has never, nor will it ever, prevail against it.

With great respect, yours,

KIRWAN.

LETTER VI.

Popery has degraded Ireland—Evidences of its degradation—Absenteeism—Sub-letting—Tithes—The priest's cry for money.

My dear Sir,—In my last letter, in which I sought to illustrate that the influence of Popery is to make the masses superstitious, and the intelligent, infidels, in all the countries where it predominates, I made the following assertion: "it has rendered our noble-hearted, noble-minded, impulsive countrymen, the hewers of wood and the drawers of water, in all the countries to which they emigrate. The degradation of Ireland which has made it a by-word, I charge upon Popery." To some of the evidences of the truth of these assertions I wish to call your attention in the present letter. Perhaps the present state of feeling in our country towards famine-stricken Ireland may secure for what I shall say to you some attention.

That Ireland is a degraded country, as to its masses, with all our pride of country, neither you nor I can deny. Its general poverty, its pervading ignorance, its mud hovels, its innumerable beggars, its insubordination, are the sad and tangible proofs of its degradation. They lie upon the surface of the country, where every traveller can behold them. And the untravelled American has the evidences of this degradation brought to his own door. He sees it in the perfect ignorance of his Irish servant—in the squalid appearance of the Irish beggar—in the deep-rooted superstition of the Irish papist—in the Irish brawls in low tippling-houses—in the furious passions of an Irish mob—in the large proportion of Irish convicts in our prisons, and of vicious Irish in our places of moral reform. It is, my dear sir, with feelings of regret and shame that I make this statement. My love of country has never forsaken me for an hour. With all its faults, I love Ireland still; and in the lowest depths of their degradation its children manifest a sensibility and a nobility that would honor those in the highest ranks of civilization, and that evince what they would be under a right development of their social and moral nature. What are the causes of this degradation?

I will not, I cannot omit from the list of causes what is technically called Absenteeism: the lordly proprietors of the land living in foreign countries, and expending abroad the hard earnings of their tenants at home. This is one of the grievous curses of Ireland.

Nor can I omit the system of letting and sub-letting, or renting and sub-renting of the land, by the richer to the less rich, until between the owner and the actual cultivator there may be six to twelve landlords, each living upon those below him; and the actual tillers of the land supporting them all! This is infusing into the curse of absenteeism an ingredient which multiplies its bitterness by ten. It gives rise to a class of landlords as unpitying as famine.

Nor can I omit the system of tithes for the support of the Established Church of Ireland. An Episcopal priest is placed in every parish in Ireland; and if he has not one single parishioner to wait on his ministrations, he is yet entitled to his tithes from the parish. And these tithes are drawn from the actual cultivators of the soil, the poor tenants. And these tithes are usually let and sublet, as is the land; and their collection usually falls into the hands of men as rapacious as vultures. Yes, and the priest for whose support these tithes are paid may never have made the impress of his foot upon the soil of his parish! Yes, and when the tither calls upon the poor man to pay his tithes for the support of a minister he has never seen, and for the maintenance of a religion which his soul abhors, unless he is ready to pay, his only cow, more than one half the support of his family, is driven to the market and there sold for half her value! And if that does not pay, his pig is driven and sold in the same way! Such is the system of tithes in Ireland! I have no language, my dear sir, in which to express my abhorrence of it. The support of such a system is a disgrace to the Protestant name, it is a deep, dark, direful stain upon the equity of British legislation. It is a public protest before heaven and earth against the church that sanctions it, and against the craven-hearted, earthly-minded clergy that can submit to be thus supported! Out of your own church, sir, I know of no ecclesiastical nuisance so utterly offensive as that of the Established Church of Ireland! And yet the very upholders of these schemes of robbery, yes, and some of the very individuals that pocket the plunder thus legally and ecclesiastically filched from the poor people, write to us about public faith and honesty, and lecture us upon the subject of slavery as if they were spotless as Gabriel! Of all this I can say, as Talleyrand is reported to have said of a lady that frequently annoyed him; "Madam," said he, "you have but one fault." "Pray, sir," said she, "what is it?" "It is," said he, "that you are perfectly insufferable." Nor have I seen, among the various plans suggested by Lord John Russell for the relief of Ireland, a hint at the abolition of this nefarious system of tithes.

Bad, my dear sir, as I think of these causes, and much as they have contributed to the degradation and impoverishing of Ireland, they are but as the dust of the balance when compared with the influences of Popery. And that yourself may see this, hear me to the close, calmly, and without prejudice.

Why this Absenteeism, of which we so bitterly and justly complain? I am not about to excuse it; but one of its reasons is the opposition of the priest to the efforts of the land proprietor to elevate his tenantry, and the fierce jealousies which the priest excites in the minds of the people. There is but little Absenteeism in Scotland; why is it so general in Ireland? The cause we find in the difference of the religion of the two people. If the parish priest of Ireland was like the parish minister of Scotland, the Marquis of Sligo would have as pleasant a home upon his estate as the Duke of Buccleugh, or the Marquis of Broadalbane.

Popery does nothing for the education of the people of Ireland. With the wealth of the middling classes under its control, and almost at its beck, where are its schools and its colleges for the education of its people? You send to Ireland for money to establish them here; why erect none there? Connaught, where your church has complete control, is an almost unbroken mass of ignorance. And Munster is precisely like it. And these are the portions of it where the famine is now raging. Ignorance brutalizes, and sensualizes, and renders men improvident. It places our higher in subjection to our lower nature; and in withholding education from the people popery has degraded Ireland. And wherever its children are carried by the tide of emigration, their want of education places them in the lowest grade of society: and they are more dreaded as a burden, than hailed as an accession. Without the high aspirations which knowledge imparts, and without the self-respect which it creates, they are satisfied with being menials where they might be masters—to be carriers of mortar, where they might be chief builders on the wall. If the ignorance of Ireland has any thing to do with the degradation of Ireland, *I charge that ignorance upon Popery.*

And if Absenteeism, and sub-letting, and the tithe system do much to impoverish the people, Popery does yet more. It meets them at the cradle, and dogs them to the grave, and beyond it, with its demands for money. When the child is baptized, the priest must have money. When the mother is churched, the priest must have money. When the boy is confirmed, the bishop must have money. When he goes to confession, the priest must have money. When he partakes of the Eucharist, the priest must have money. When visited in sickness, the priest must have money. If he wants a charm against sickness or the witches, he must pay for it money. When he is buried, his friends must pay money. After mass is said over his remains, a plate is placed on the coffin, and the people collected together on the occasion are expected to deposit their contribution on the plate. Then the priest pockets the money, and the people take the body to the grave. And then, however good the person, his soul has gone to Purgatory ; and however bad, his soul may have stopped there. And then comes the money for prayers and masses for deliverance from purgatory, which prayers and masses are continued as long as the money continues to be paid. Now when we remember that seven out of the nine millions of the people of Ireland are papists, and of the most bigoted stamp; and that this horse-leech process of collecting money, whose ceaseless cry is "*give, give*," is in operation in every parish; and that as far as possible every individual is subjected to it, can we wonder at the poverty and the degradation of Ireland? Can we wonder that its noble-hearted, noble-minded people, are every where hewers of wood and drawers of water? Shame, shame, upon your church, that it treats a people so confiding and faithful so basely! Shame, shame upon it, that it does so little to elevate a people that contribute so freely to its support! O, Popery, thou hast debased my country—thou hast impoverished its people—thou hast enslaved its mind! From the hodman on the ladder—from the digger of the canal—from the ostler in the stable—from the unlettered cook in the kitchen, and the maid in the parlor—from the rioter in the street—from the culprit at the bar—from the state prisoner in his lonely dungeon—from the victim of a righteous law stepping into eternity from the gallows, for a murder committed under the delirium of passion or whisky, I hear a protest against thee as the great cause of the deep degradation of as noble a people as any upon which the sun shines in the circuit of its glorious way!

My dear sir, your religion is for the benefit of the priest, and not that of the people. Its object is not to spread light, but darkness,—not to advance civilization but to retard it,—not to elevate but to depress man, that he may the more readily be brought under your influence. And we have in Ireland a type of what our happy land will be when the priest wields the power here which he wields there.

I own, dear sir, that I have digressed a little from my original object in these letters. But in my next I shall commence with the reasons which on the most mature reflection yet prevent me from returning to the pale of your church.

With great respect, yours,

Kir

LETTER VII.

Reasons for not returning to the papal church—Prohibition of the Scriptures—The way and manner of papal worship—Ceremonial law of popery—Obstructions raised between God and the soul

My dear Sir,—Agreeably to the promise made to you in my last letter, I now commence a statement of the reasons which, on the most mature reflection, yet prevent me from returning to the pale of your church. I wish to avoid prolixity of statement, and minuteness of detail; as I feel that I am addressing one who can see the point, and weigh the force of an argument, without either.

When, in the kind providence of God, my mind became interested to know what God would have me to do, I cast around for a true guide to the solution of the question. Where could I find such an one? Books are written by fallible men—priests had already imposed on my understanding—fond parents, deceived themselves, taught me superstition for religion—all men are liable to err. I felt there was a God, and that I was bound to obey him; but where is the rule of my obedience? This was *the* question. I was told of the Bible, but of that I knew nothing; and, then, I knew the Bible to be by your church a prohibited book, or to be read only by priestly permission. I sought the Bible, and read it. I found it to be the true, and only guide to the right solution of the question as to what God would have me to do. And without the fear of the Pope, or of the anathemas of the Council of Trent, and without a line of license from prelate or priest, I have continued to read it for years. And the virtual prohibition of the unfettered reading of the Bible by your church, is one of the main reasons why I cannot return to it. That your restrictions amount to a virtual prohibition your candor, will not for a moment deny.

And let me ask you, dear sir, why this virtual prohibition? Who has given you authority to say that I must not read what God has given to direct me into all the ways of faith and obedience? God has commanded me to "Search the Scriptures;" who has *given you authority to forbid me?* What right have you to forbid me, more than I have to forbid you? Produce your credentials! Where does God place his Revealed Will in the keeping of pope, prelate or priest, to be doled out to his erring children in such ways and parcels as they may deem best? He has no more placed the Bible under your control, or that of your church, than he has the sun in heaven, or the vital air. Nor can I conceive of any principle that can possibly induce you to withhold it from the people, without gloss or comment, save one: "Every one that doeth evil hateth the light, neither cometh to light, lest his deeds should be reproved." It is said that Herod, when convinced that he was not of the royal line of the

Jews, burned their genealogies and records, that his false pretences might not be confuted by them. Is it for a similar reason that your church withholds the Bible from the people? The Bible lays the axe at the root of the Upas tree of Popery; is this the reason why it is withheld?

Another of the reasons which prevent me from returning to your church is the way and the manner of your public worship of God. On reading the New Testament, I find that Jesus Christ embraced every opportunity of declaring the will of God. After his ascension and the descent of the Spirit, the Apostles went every where preaching the gospel of the Kingdom. The worship of God as taught us in the New Testament, consists in prayer, praise, and the preaching of his word for the instruction and edification of his people. To the instruction and edification of the saints every thing in the church of Christ is made subservient. Is it so in the church of Rome? Do your Masses convey any instruction to the common or the uncommon mind? Do they ever give, have they ever given, one true idea of God, or of religion, to a human soul? If so I should like to know it. May not individuals attend upon them from youth to gray hairs, and yet know not the first principles of the doctrines of Christ? I have attended recently, sir, a High Mass at one of your Cathedrals. It was on the last Christmas day. I bore the unmeaning pageant for three nours together. There was the bishop in his robes, with his cap, his crook and his crosier—there were priests, in numbers, moving about, making their crosses, obeisances and genuflexions—when the bishop rose, the cross and crosier moved before him, and the priests, as waiters, went behind him—the book was shifted from side to side, and was read and chanted in ways that no mortal hearer could comprehend—there was the raising of the Host, and the bowing down of the people—the incense, and all the other usual accompaniments of such a service; and it struck me as one of the most farcical pantomines that I ever witnessed. I left the house without receiving a solitary religious suggestion, and puzzled and confounded for a solution to the question, how intelligent men could possibly submit to act such a farce, and to pass it off upon a crowd of poor looking people for the solemn worship of God? And if your Mass, when thus performed with all the splendor and pomp of your ritual, is thus unmeaning, how insipid must it be when performed in your country chapels by ignorant priests, who hunt up the sheep only to shear off their wool! God, my dear sir, is an intelligent God, he has given me intelligence with which to worship him. For the intelligence within me, either as to its increase or exercise, your church makes no provision in its public worship. I must not, then, return to your church, and seek to have my soul, made for the inhabitation of the Spirit, satisfied with the mummery of your muttered Masses, in the public worship of my God.

Another of the reasons which prevent me from returning to your church is, the burdens which it places on my conscience, which crush, without correcting it. It institutes a kind of a ceremonial law which restricts where God has given liberty; and which licenses where God has prohibited indulgence. With your Fast and Feast days, who can keep up without an almanac in his hand? And how many of your people can read it? Should I blunder in counting the days of the week, and, mistaking Friday for Thursday, eat meat, my conscience is wounded. If in performing penance I miscount my beads, and say a less number of Pater Nosters than required, my conscience again suffers. If, ignorant of the "Laws of Lent" which have been just published by you, I should eat three meals on a day between "Ash Wednesday and Easter Sunday," or should eat meat on the "Thursday next after Ash Wednesday," or on "any day in the Holy Week," my conscience would be again burdened. And these are but specimens of the thousand and one ceremonial regulations of your church, as burdensome as they are unmeaning, which fret and crush the conscience without directing or strengthening it. And whilst thus restricted in things indifferent, I am freely indulged in things which the divine law prohibits.

Now, sir, who has given you authority to make laws where God has made none? Where is the law in the Statute Book for your Lents, your Feast days, your Fast days, your Easter days? Why fast or feast at one time more than another? Who has given you authority to say what I shall eat, or how often, in any one day of the year? What unutterable arrogance to tell me I cannot eat fish and flesh at the same meal; what priestly intolerance to tell me, with my Bible open before me, that if I transgress these laws I sin against my God! You know that the gospel is a law of liberty, you know that if a man eat meat he is not the worse, and that if he refrain he is not the better—you know that the Bible teaches that man is defiled, not by that which entereth into him, but by that which cometh out of him. And why burden souls and fetter consciences by silly enactments about things in themselves indifferent, and about which God has made no regulations? O, sir, like the Scribes and the Pharisees of old, you are busied about the mint, the annis and the cumin, forgetful of the weightier matters of the law. And I deeply regret that a man who has forced himself up to station and influence against so many adverse circumstances, had not force enough left to break the chains of early religious prejudice, to rise up to the region of intellectual, and moral, and religious freedom! You are too much of a man to stoop to such nonsense. I would leave such things to those who know no better.

On these subjects, dear sir, your church must return to the standard of the Bible, and of common sense, before I can return to it.

Another of the reasons which prevent my return is, the obstructions which your church raises between me and my God. My Bible, that hated book by pope, prelate, priest and papal peasant, teaches me that if any man sin he has an Advocate with the Father—Jesus Christ. It every where teaches me, that I may have free access to God through Jesus Christ, that if I sin, I may go for pardon directly to the throne of God, through the mediation of his Son. And this is a precious privilege; a privilege which may be enjoyed by all, "*without money and without price.*" Now what do you ask of me to do in order to receive the forgiveness of sin, and to be restored to the favor of God? You send me to Peter or Paul, or some other saint on the catalogue, who may have never known me; and who may never hear me, if I pray unto them. Or you send me to Mary, whom you blasphemously call the Mother of God, to ask her to intercede for me. Nor will this suffice. I must go to your Confessional, and tell you *all* my sins; incurring the fearful penalty of refusal of pardon if I withhold one. Thus you take from me the privilege of going to God for myself, a privilege purchased for me by the death of Christ. You tell me I must go to the priest; and from the priest to the saint, or to the Virgin; and the Saint or Virgin will go for me to the Saviour; and he will go for me to the Father And then when pardon is granted, it goes from the Father to the Son—from him to the Saint or Virgin —from him or her to the priest; and when in the hands of the priest, he will give me absolution, *if I pay for it!* Will you say, dare you say, that this is a caricature of your teachings upon this matter? Would to God you could, with truth! Why send me to the saints to ask them to intercede for me, if this is untrue? That I am a sinner, I know and feel. That there is pardon for me through the atonement of Jesus Christ, on my repentance and faith, is a precious doctrine of the Bible, and of my creed. That pardon I receive the moment I sincerely exercise the graces of repentance and faith; —yes, and not a whit the less freely, if all of you, pope, patriarchs, prelates and priests, were with Pharaoh and his chariots.

And why turn me away from the door of mercy, and compel me to speak to my heavenly Father by proxy? Why call me away from the cross, and send me to a priest, or a saint, or a virgin, to ask them to do for me what I can better do for myself? Where has my Saviour taught me that I can only address him through a priestly attorney, that I must fee, however poor, for his services? O, ask me to do any thing—to bale the ocean—to tame the hurricane—to arrest the sun—rather than ask me to return to your church, until every thing is removed which forbids the free access of my soul to my God,

—which suspends my salvation on any thing else than repentance towards God, and faith in our Lord Jesus Christ. You must pull down your toll-gates on the way of life, before you see me back.

The statement of a few additional reasons I hope to give you in my next.

With great respect, yours,

KIRWAN.

LETTER VIII.

Farther reasons for not returning to the papal church—Celibacy of the clergy—Auricular confessions—A call on Irish papists to assert their rights.

MY DEAR SIR,—In my last letter I entered on the statement of the reasons which yet prevent me from returning to the pale of your church. I adverted only to four: your virtual prohibition of the Bible; the way and manner of your public worship of God;—your ceremonial law, which burdens and crushes, without instructing or correcting the conscience; and the obstructions which you erect between my soul and my God. These, or either of them, would be reason sufficient not merely to excuse, but to forbid, my ever returning to your communion. For me to give farther reasons would seem to be a little like your doctrine of Supererogation, which is not among the least of the absurd errors of your infallible church; but as the argument is cumulative, you will bear with me whilst I proceed to the statement of a few others.

I cannot return to your church, until you cease teaching for doctrines the commandments of men Permit me here to say, dear sir, that, without a solitary exception, the things which are peculiar to your church,—the things which make it distinctively what it is, are the commandments of men, either in direct opposition to the teachings of the Bible, or based upon the most gross perversion of its meaning. In as brief a manner as possible, permit me to illustrate this position.

Your church teaches and enjoins the celibacy of its clergy, in language the most pointed and positive; and the Council of Trent hurls its anathemas against all who would assert the contrary doctrine, or who would admit the lawfulness of the marriage of a priest. Thus you forbid the priest to marry—you damn him if he does marry—and you anathematize all who think or say that in marrying he sinned not against God or man. All this, you admit, is so. Now, then, I ask your authority for so teaching. I ask not your ecclesiastical, but your scriptural authority. Did not the Jewish priests marry? Was not Peter your first pope? This you assert. And was not Peter's wife's mother sick of a fever? Matt. 8: 14. Pope Peter, then, had a wife. Why would it be a mortal sin in pope Pius IX. to have one also? Would he be the less pious or moral on that account? You, sir, are a bishop.

How far you are a scriptural bishop, is not now the inquiry. But Paul in writing to Timothy says, "A bishop *must* be the husband of one wife . . . . having his children in subjection with all gravity." And even poor "deacons," the lowest order of your ministry, are thus instructed by Paul, "Let the deacons be the husbands of one wife, ruling their children and their own houses well." 1 Tim. 3: 12.

Now, dear sir, put these things together, and see in what a position they place you! Peter, your first pope, had a wife; and you damn to the depths of perdition any pope that would, in this respect, follow pope Peter! Challoner says that he had no commerce with his wife after he was made an apostle!! Will you tell me how Challoner found that out? Deacons and bishops *are commanded*, or at least permitted to have wives, and you would empty the seven vials of your wrath, and pour all the anathemas of Trent upon the head of the priest or bishop that, in obeying God, would disobey your church! Is it possible for you and the Bible to be in more direct opposition? Is it wrong to conclude that, in thus forbidding to marry, your church gives at least one evidence that it is the Antichrist? Will you favor me, dear sir, with a common-sense exposition of the meaning of Paul, 1 Tim. 4: 3, where he brands "forbidding to marry" as a doctrine of "devils?" If half as literal in the exposition of Paul, as in your exposition of, "this is my body," "this is my blood," how will you avoid the inference that you are a devil?

Again; your church enjoins confession, under the most stringent rules. To this I have already adverted in former letters. I advert to it again to illustrate how you teach for doctrines the commandments of men. The Council of Trent teaches that "it is the duty of every man who hath fallen after baptism to confess his sins at least once a year to a priest." It teaches that "this confession of sin is to be secret, for public confession is neither commanded nor expedient." It teaches that "this confession of sin must be very exact and particular, together with all circumstances, and that it extend to the most secret sins, even of thought or against the 9th or 10th Commandment." You know you omit the 2nd Commandment which forbids your bowing to pictures and images, and divide the 10th into two, so as to make up the 9th and 10th, and thus complete the number. On receiving confession as thus ordained, the priest pronounces absolution upon the penitent, "not conditional or declarative only, but absolute and judicial." When I remember the use which your church has made of this doctrine, and the fearful power which it gives the priest over the people, my heart swells with emotion as I pen these lines; and, like the angel of Manoah's sacrifice, my thanksgivings ascend to heaven, that I have escaped the snare of the fowler.

Now, Sir, let me again turn querist and ask you where in the Bible do you find your doctrine of confession taught? With me the teachings of all your Councils weigh not a feather; give me, if you can, Bible authority. Is there one text from Genesis to Revelation, which you, as a scholar, will say teaches it? I put this question to you, not as a bishop, but as a scholar. A priest from Maynooth, taught there only to mumble the Missal; or a poor unlettered peasant from Mayo or Galway, into whose lips words are put, as into the mouth of a parrot, might quote to me James v. 16, which says, "Confess your faults one to another;" but will *you* do it? They might tell me that the Pharisees were baptized of John Baptist, "confessing their sins"—that at Ephesus, "many that believed came and confessed, and showed their deeds"—but will *you* do it? If James is your authority, are not you bound to confess to me, if I am to you? "Confess your faults *one to another;*"—if this text teaches auricular confession, I hold you to it. When did you put the poor Irishman, who whispered his sins into your ears. in your seat in the Confessional, and kneeling down outside, whisper through the little square hole cut in its side, your sins into his ear? This would be *confessing your sins one to another.* Did you ever do this, Sir? Never, never. I ask you again, not as a bishop, but as a scholar, whether a single text quoted by Challoner, or Butler, or Hay, gives a shadow of countenance to your doctrine of confession?

Lay aside your mitre, your crosier, your crook, and your canonicals, and look at those texts as simple John Hughes, and then answer my question. How can you account to man or to God for the erection of such an awful institution as Auricular Confession, upon the merest perversion of Scripture, a perversion which has neither sense nor wit to excuse it, and without a solitary text or example in the Bible to sustain it? O, why will you do as a priest, what you would not do as a scholar, or as a man?

And, then, what aggravates the whole matter is, that every man who is made a priest, no matter how ignorant or wicked, feels himself divinely appointed of heaven to confess sinners, and to absolve them from their sins! No matter if he is a Judas, he has the same authority to confess and absolve as Peter! A priest, Sir, under your own jurisdiction, and I am sorry to say, an Irishman also, was heard thus to address the ostler of the hotel at which he boarded, on returning from Mass on Sabbath afternoon, "Pat, get up my horse, I have to go and confess a poor devil who is dying five or six miles out in the country." I would not say this wretch is a fair sample of all your priests: I hope otherwise. But there are too many like him! And he has the same power to confess and absolve that you have, against whose character I know nothing, save that you sustain a system which you must know to be as false as the Koran.

I would implore you, my dear sir, to review this

doctrine of your church. As to the word of God it is baseless as the fabric of a vision. It was unknown in the Jewish church; it is untaught in the Christian Scriptures. It crept into your church during the dark ages. It was nailed upon it at Trent. It is clearly a device of man, and in terrible opposition to some of the plainest precepts of God's word. It gives power to the priest, and enslaves the people. It has been to your church, in every land, a fearful source of corruption. Every thing is beneath you but the truth. Reject the lie, however long it may have been told, and however it may increase your income and influence. No longer prostitute your fine talents and education in maintaining this religious juggle, but send the sinner to the cross, telling him that whosoever shall there confess and forsake his sin, shall find mercy. In this thing show yourself a man; and the blessings of unborn generations will be upon you.

And could I address myself to every papist upon whom the sun shines, I would say to them all, and especially to those of your country and mine, *the doctrine of confession is a priestly device to gain an absolute authority over your consciences.* You are no more bound to confess to a priest, than he is to confess to you. And as to the doctrine of Absolution, connected with Confession, it is simply blasphemy. God only can forgive sin. And were it not for the fees connected with your Confession and Absolution, there is not a priest upon the face of the earth that would care a straw about your Confession, or that would commit the blasphemy of forgiving your sins. If bishops or priests will not, in this day of light, cut in pieces the net wove in the dark ages to confine and trammel you, it is in your power to rise and tear it in pieces. Irish Roman Catholics! our fathers fought and bled and died, to obtain for themselves and for us civil liberty. Their blood shed by British bayonets in these struggles for their civil rights, have crimsoned every stream and fattened every field of Ireland. And will you, their sons, bow your necks to a priestly tyranny, which debases you mentally and morally? Will you give yourselves to be led, and rode, and robbed, by priests who come to you pretending that the keys of heaven hang by their girdle, and that it is with them to let you in, or shut you out at pleasure? No man can be a slave whilst his soul is free; nor can any man be free, whilst his soul is in bondage.

There is, Rev. sir, one confession which I freely make to you; my spirit waxes warm when I think or write upon the absurdities of your church—upon its flagrant perversions of the Scriptures—upon its shameful impositions upon the ignorant and credulous—upon the unblushing effrontery with which it teaches for divine doctrines the commandments of men. And I assure you that my warmth of feeling is not diminished when I consider that a man of your character and country, could consent to be a chief workman in this bad business. Irishmen have their faults; but they are not usually those of duplicity, or perversion of the truth. And, hence, whilst they may make good papists, they make bad Jesuits.

I regret to find that I must end this letter without ending my illustrations of the way and manner in which you teach for doctrines the commandments of men. This I hope to do in my next.

With great respect, yours,

KIRWAN.

LETTER IX.

Reasons which prevent from returning to the papal church continued—Purgatory—Transubstantiation.

MY DEAR SIR,—I will proceed with the statement of the reasons which prevent me from returning to the pale of your church. I have reached my fifth reason; your teaching for doctrines of divine authority the commandments of men. I entered upon the illustration of the way in which you do this in my last, and without ending my illustrations ended my letter. Permit me to state a few more, for your candid consideration.

The doctrine of Purgatory is one of the peculiar doctrines of your church. You teach that nearly all Christians when they die are "neither so perfectly pure and clean as to exempt them from the least spot or stain; nor yet so unhappy as to die under the guilt of unrepented deadly sin." It is for these *middling* Christians that you make a purgatory, where they remain until they make full satisfaction for sin; and then they go to heaven. And the "Profession of Faith" of Pius IV. tells us "that the souls therein detained are helped by the suffrages of the faithful; that is, by the prayers and the alms offered for them, and principally by the holy sacrifice of the Mass." And the doctrine of your church is so expounded upon this matter that but few, if any, die, however good, without needing purgatorial purification; and that but few are so bad but that they may be there fitted for heaven. This you will admit is a fair statement. The more you get into purgatory, the more you will receive of the "suffrages of the faithful," that is, of their money.

I have already told you my estimate of this doctrine. It is that by which your church traffics in the souls of men; and an amazingly profitable traffic it makes of it. It has placed in your possession riches far exceeding in value the mines of Peru. And because of the *value* of this doctrine you seek in all possible ways to sustain it. With me the authority of your popes and councils is not worth a penny. I would rather have one text of Scripture bearing upon the point than the teachings of as many such as you could string between here and Jupiter. Let us then look at the chief texts adduced to sustain a purgatory.

One of these texts is Matt. 12 : 32: "Whosoever speaketh against the Holy Ghost it shall not be forgiven him, neither in this world, neither in the world to come." Matt. 5 : 26 is another: "Verily I say unto thee, thou shalt by no means come out thence till thou hast paid the uttermost farthing." Both these, you say, refer to purgatory. From the one you conclude that sins may be forgiven in the next world—from the other, that none can get out of purgatory till the last farthing is paid. Now, dear sir, let me ask you, how you put these texts together? If sins are forgiven, how or why is payment also required to the last farthing? Can I forgive a debt and yet require its payment? Look at the first text again; you find purgatory in it, but how? In this way; because there is a sin which will not be forgiven in this world nor in the world to come, *therefore* there is a sin that will be forgiven in the world to come!! Such is the logic of infallible Rome! Because a certain sin is not to be forgiven here or hereafter, *therefore* many sins will be forgiven hereafter! And because "this world" and "the world to come" is inclusive of all time and place, Popery builds up a place which belongs neither to this world nor to the world to come, and fills it with fire, and calls it Purgatory! Like Mahomet's coffin, it floats somewhere between heaven and hell. Into this world of fire you drive the souls of men as they leave the body, and let them out only on the reception of "the suffrages of the faithful"—that is, their money! Now, sir, what do you say to all this?

But, you ask, are there not other texts quoted by our writers to sustain Purgatory as a Scriptural institution? O yes, but they are as far from the point as the most vivid imagination can well conceive. They are by the diameter of the heavens farther from the point, than those just quoted. Let any intelligent man read chapter xiv. of Challoner's "Catholic Christian," and he will rise from it with amazement that God could ever leave men to the folly of so perverting Scripture; or that even the devil could permit them so absurdly to misapply it. Permit me to quote an instance by way of illustration. We are taught in Matt. 12: 36, that we must give an account for *every idle word* in the day of judgment. Now how does this text prove a Purgatory? In this wise: "No one can think that God will condemn a soul to hell for every idle word; *therefore* there must be a purgatory to punish those guilty of these little transgressions." If you or any mortal man, think I am joking, let him turn to the chapter. Let me quote the answer in full to the question, Are not souls in Purgatory capable of relief in that state? "Yes, they are, but not for any thing that they can do for themselves, but from the prayers, *alms, and other suffrages offered to God* for them by the faithful upon earth, which *God in his mercy is pleased to accept of*, by reason of that communion which we have with them, by being fellow members of the same body of the Church, under the same head, which is Jesus Christ." Now, sir, if in this answer you substitute the word "priest" for "God," then we come to the facts in the case. The "alms" and the other "suffrages of the faithful," are pocketed by the priest. And purgatory was invented for the special purpose of securing these alms, and other suffrages of the faithful, to pope, prelates, and priests.

Now, sir, let me ask you a few questions. Perhaps I have asked you too many already; but you will bear with a fellow-countryman, anxious, not so much to embarrass you, as to bring out the truth. What has the blood of Christ, which cleanses *from all sin*, to do with the venial sins of those middling Christians who die, not good enough to go to heaven, nor bad enough to go to hell? What has the blood of Christ, his atonement, his finished work, at all to do, on your plan, with the saving of the sinner? If my child should die and go to purgatory, would a thousand dollars given to you at once, have the same effect as a hundred dollars a year for ten years? How can you tell when enough is given to get the soul out; or has your purse no bottom? As souls are spirits without bodies, how can you tell one soul from another as they issue from the gates of purgatory? In the prayer "Hail Mary," we are made to utter at its conclusion, the following petition: "Holy Mary, Mother of God, pray for us sinners, now and *at the hour of our death*;" why not solicit her to pray for us *after our death*, to get us out of purgatory? Is it because you are afraid the good woman would get us out before the priests had gotten enough of the "alms and suffrages of the faithful?"

My dear sir, the absurdities connected with your doctrine of purgatory are sickening. It is based on the love of money. The bishop of Air candidly confesses that it is not revealed in the Scriptures. It came into the church in the seventh century, it was affirmed in the twelfth;—it was stereotyped at Trent; and fearful anathemas are hurled at all who deny it. It puts away the work of Jesus Christ, and sends the sinner, not to "the blood of sprinkling," but to the fire of purgatory, in order to secure a meetness for heaven. And why this parody—this caricature of the religion of God? Simply to put "the alms and the suffrages of the faithful" in the pockets of your priests! What an outrage upon the common sense of the world to have men, dressed up in canonicals, teaching things as true, of which the beast that Balaam rode might well be ashamed!

I entreat you, my dear sir, to review this doctrine of your church. *You*, surely, must see its absurdity. Neither in the word of God, nor in the common reason of man, is there the shadow of an argument to sustain it. Nor is there a class of men upon the face of the earth who deserve a purgatory from which "the alms and other suffrages of the faithful" would never release them, as do those who preach up a purgatory and its fearful torments, for the sake of filthy lucre. But, as Father O'Leary said to Canning, "I am afraid many of them will go farther and fare worse." My high respect for you renders me solicitous that you should not be of the number. I wish you not to be one of the dumb herd who hold the truth in unrighteousness, and believe a lie that they may be damned.

Transubstantiation is another of the peculiar doctrines of your church. By this you teach, that, in the Lord's Supper, the bread and the wine are converted into the real body and blood of Christ, by the consecration of the priest. The thing is so absurd as to confute itself; and as, therefore, to require from me but a brief statement. Challoner, Chap. V., thus states the doctrine: "The bread and wine are changed by the consecration into the body and blood of Christ." "Is it then the belief of the Church that Jesus Christ himself, true God and true man, is truly, really, and substantially present in the blessed sacrament? It is, for where the body and blood of Christ are, there his soul also and his divinity needs be. And consequently there must be whole Christ, God and man: there is no taking him to pieces." And all this is proven to demonstration by the quoting of the words of Christ at the institution of the Supper, "This is my body," "This is my blood."

Now, sir, if you and your church had only the common sense to look for the true meaning of the two little words "is" and "this" in the above sentences of the Saviour, it would have saved you a world of trouble. Look at one or two similar passages: "The seven good kine are seven years—and the seven good ears are seven years."—Gen. 41: 26. "The seven stars are the angels of the seven churches."—Rev. 1: 20. "The seven heads are the seven mountains."—Rev. 17: 9. The sense is plain here. They *signify* those things. So the word "is" may mean to *signify*. Now for the word "this." It obviously refers to the bread. I will have none of your nonsense about "the substance contained under the species." It is darkening counsel by words without knowledge. So that the simple, natural, reasonable, scriptural sense is: "This bread signifies or represents my body"—"This wine signifies or represents my blood." Just see how a little common sense simplifies every thing!

Now, turning back to your interpretation, permit me in view of it to ask you a few questions: Did the apostles at the first institution of the Supper, eat the real body and blood of Christ? So your church must and does teach! What power have you, more than I have, to work such a miracle as to change a little wafer into the real body and blood of Christ? If you stickle so much for the letter in your interpretation of "This is my body," "This is my blood," why withhold the wine from all but the priests? Why give up the bread for a wafer? If some wag should mix arsenic with the wafer before consecration, would you be willing to take it after you had changed it into the real body and blood of Christ? You place great dependence on John 6 : 56. You take it literally. Will you take the whole connection literally? Then he that eateth this bread *shall live for ever*. He that eats this bread *will never hunger*. All that you have to do, if your principle is true, is to give your wafer to the poor, famishing Irish, and they hunger no more!

But the thing is too outrageously absurd to dwell upon! Nothing equals it in absurdity in all paganism. If a man should mumble a few words over a stone, and tell you it was converted by these words into bread, what would you say to him? If, against all the evidences of your senses, he should seriously assert that it was bread;—and if, in addition, he should seriously assert that unless you believed that stone to be bread you must be damned, would you not be for putting him in a strait jacket?

But I must bring this letter to a close. These are but a few of the illustrations of the way and manner in which you teach for doctrines the commandments of men. And without at all exhausting the subject, I must here close my statement of the reasons which forbid me to return to the pale of your church. When I give up my Bible for the commandments of men, they must have learning, or genius, or wit, or something to recommend them.

They must be, at least, good nonsense, which, you know, to an Irishman is quite interesting.

With great respect, yours,

KIRWAN.

LETTER X.

Is the Church of Rome a Church of Christ?

MY DEAR SIR,—I have with all frankness and honesty stated to you the reasons which yet prevent me from returning to the pale of your church. And although I have stated but five, which are scarcely a tithe of those that press themselves forward for utterance, yet, if not to you, they are to myself and I think are to all unbiassed minds entirely sufficient. I have even the faith to believe that you yourself will deem them sufficient; and that were it not for the peculiarity of your position, and your plighted oath, to sustain your church, right or wrong, that they would have the same effect upon your mind and conduct that they have upon mine.

Whilst reviewing and weighing these reasons, the questions have arisen before my mind, Is the Roman Catholic, a church of Christ? Has it so far departed from the truth, or so grievously perverted it, as to forfeit all claim to that title? These are questions of grave import, which I will not undertake to decide. But I wish to state to you in the present letter, how some things bearing on these questions strike me, and then I will submit the decision of them to yourself. To this, surely, you will make no objection.

The external organization of your church is obviously not that taught by Christ and his Apostles. As to this matter, every thing in the Bible is simple. The kingdom of Christ is not of outward observation—its seat is in the hearts and affections of men—its elements are righteousness, and peace, and joy in the Holy Ghost. The great object of the Apostles and first preachers of the doctrines of Christ was to win men to the belief and to the practice of the truth. When men believed the truth, they were baptized, and were thus introduced into the communion of the saints; and not a word is said about popes, patriarchs, cardinals, metropolitans, prelates, or of the duty of implicit obedience to their authority. There is a government enjoined, but it is as free and as simple as one can well conceive; whilst yours is as despotic, and as absurdly pompous as one can well imagine. As your external organization is not taught in the Bible, where did you get it?

The answer to this question to my mind is plain. As the early Church advanced in numbers, influence, and wealth, it gradually lost the martyr spirit of its founders. Its ministers became corrupt, secular, and ambitious. By degrees, bishops, from an office, became an order. As Rome was the metropolis of the world, and it was there that the greatest number of martyrs had shed their blood, the bishop of the metropolitan city soon became pre-eminent among his brethren. Now the State sought the influence of the church to assist in maintaining its authority; and the church sought the influence of the State to assist in building up its ghostly dominion. Each yielded to the request of the other. The church rapidly extended; and the ambition of priests conceived the idea of governing it after the model of the state. Rome must be the centre of ecclesiastical as of civil power. The State had its Cæsar,—the church must have its pope. Cæsar had his governors of provinces,—the pope must have his patriarchs. The governors had their subordinates; and these again theirs, down to the very lowest office; so that the patriarchs had their archbishops; these their bishops; and these their priests; and so down to the very lowest office in the church. As in the State all civil authority emanated from Cæsar, and all disputes were finally referable to him; so in the church all ecclesiastical authority emanated from the pope, and he was made the final judge of all disputes. Here, sir, is the origin of your ecclesiastical government. And did the limits of a letter permit, I could run out this parallel into some details which even to you would be striking and confounding. Your ecclesiastical organization has just the same divine warrant that that of Mahometanism, or Hindooism has,—God permits it. The Roman Empire has passed away; ages ago its mangled limbs were strewn over the earth. But in that ecclesiastical organization called Popery, we have the living model of that form of government by which the Cæsars bound the nations of the earth to their thrones; and by which they were enabled to crush, at the extremes of the world, every effort to break the yoke of servitude.

How far all this bears upon the question, whether yours is a church of Christ, I submit to your candid decision. When weighing this matter, I would entreat you not to jeopardize your standing as a scholar and as a man of sense, by any reference to, "Thou art Peter, and upon this rock I build my church." Leave that thing to the boys from Maynooth, with long coats and short brains.

The forms and method of your public worship are obviously not those taught us in the Bible. I enter your church, Saint Patrick's, to worship God. I am required to sprinkle myself with Holy Water, and to make on myself the sign of the cross. And why, or for what purpose? That I may be defended from unclean spirits! I look around me, and I see a forest of candles burning upon the altar. And for what purpose? where is this commanded? I see people counting their beads, and praying before pictures Where is this taught? Now comes out a priest in his robes embroidered with crosses. Did Peter or Paul wear such things when teaching Jews and Gentiles the faith of Christ? He says nothing to the people, but goes through the Mass in Latin, of which I may know nothing. Was this the way Peter and Paul did? Then come out boys in white frocks, with their censers, offering incense to the priest, and filling the church with the odour. Were Peter and Paul thus incensed? The priest goes through the service, bowing, and kissing the altar, now lifting up his hands, now his eyes; now speaking in a whisper, now in full voice, according to the rules laid down. Now, Sir, where did you get these things? And after the ceremony is over, I again cross myself with Holy Water and retire. This is your public worship of God every where, and from age to age; save, that in this country there is a sermon, on sticking to Mother Church, sometimes added. Have you the most distant idea that it was in this way the first Christians worshipped God? The manner of your public worship is not scriptural, or Christian; it is heathen, and was originally adopted for the seducing of the heathen to Christianity. If Peter or Paul could be introduced to Saint Patrick's when you were going through High Mass, and were told that you were one of their successors, what would be their astonishment! What! you a successor of the men who lived by catching fish, and mending nets, and making tents!! And that farce in which you are a chief actor every Sabbath, the exact counterpart of the worship instituted by the apostles!! Your manner of public worship is not only unscriptural, but in direct opposition to scripture;—it wants nothing of heathenism but the name. And how far all this bears upon the question, whether yours is a church of Christ, I submit to your candid decision.

The Bible is God's revealed will to teach us what we should believe, and do. This Bible your church has corrupted, and labours to suppress. You mix up with the pure word of God, the Apocrypha, which lays no claim to inspiration, and whose internal evidences are fatal to such a claim. I need here only mention the recommendation of the Angel, in Tobit, *to make smoke out of the heart and liver of a fish, to scare devils out of men!* And yet this Apocrypha is of more use to you than all the Bible besides! You mutilate the ten Commandments written on stone by the finger of God! You mistranslate the Scriptures in passages innumerable, to bring out your peculiar doctrines; or to conceal its testimony against them. And where the point of Scripture cannot be broken or blunted, you put a note at the bottom in explanation. And what notes! Take the following as an illustration, appended to Rom. 4. 7. "Blessed are they whose iniquities are forgiven, and whose sins are covered." "That is, blessed are those who, by doing penance have obtained pardon and remission of their sins, and also are covered; that is, newly covered with the habit of grace, and vested with the stole of charity." Nor is the work of corruption yet done. You superadd to all this your traditions, which like a piece of Indian rubber you can stretch or contract to suit your purpose. Nor can the Bible, when all this is done, be put into promiscuous circulation, lest, with all these additions and corruptions, some might understand it as teaching some things in opposition to popery! You tell the poor Irishman that his spade and hod are better suited to him than the Bible; and the poor Irish woman that she had better keep at her broom, and wash-tub, than trouble herself about the Gospels! When you corrupt the Bible to the extent of your ability; when you add to it every thing you can, or dare:—even then you keep it from the people! Why thus fearful of the Bible?

Now, sir, how far all this bears upon the question whether yours is a church of Christ, I submit to your own decision. As far as you can, you strive to supplant the Bible as the only rule of faith; and as far as I am concerned, I would as soon strive to grope my way to heaven by the Koran, as by that which you give me as a substitute for the Bible. But I wish not to forestall your decision.

The Sacraments, instituted in condescension to our weakness, are outward and sensible signs of inward and spiritual grace. These, like the Bible, you have enlarged and corrupted. Christ and his Apostles left us but two;—you multiply them by three, and carry one. I only wonder how your ingenuity permitted you to stop at seven. Here you have allowed a Dr. Deacon, a dull Englishman, and, I believe, a Protestant in the bargain, to surpass you! He adds, *exorcism, the white garment, a taste of milk and honey*, &c. How easily you might have gone on to seven, or even seventy times seven! But in addition to multiplying, you have most grievously corrupted the two that are taught us in the New

Testament. In baptism you dip or pour three times; where is this taught? Ordinarily you permit it only to be administered in churches which have fonts, the water of which is to be blessed every year on the vigils of Easter and Whit Sunday! Where do you get this? Where is your warrant for the absurd practice of godfathers and godmothers? The priest blows three times upon the face of the person to be baptized, saying, "Depart out of him or her, O unclean spirit, and give place to the Holy Ghost";—where did you get this? He then puts a grain of blessed salt into the mouth;—then he exorcises the unclean spirit, because the devil must go out, before the person is introduced into the church! Then he wets his finger with his spittle, and touches, first, the ears, saying, "Ephphatha"—then his nostrils, saying, "unto the odour of sweetness." "Be thou put to flight, O Devil!" And when baptized, a white cloth is put on his head, and a candle in his hand. Now whence all these things? Is this a heathen ceremony, or Christian baptism?

Bad as all this is, it is strong common sense when compared with your corruption of the Lord's Supper. The bread and wine are rejected for a wafer—that wafer is converted into God—the wafer God is first worshipped, and then eaten! And to believe all this shows great exaltation of faith and piety! Some things would appear very pious were they not so absurd and ludicrous.

Now, sir, how far this multiplication and corruption of the sacraments of the Christian religion enters into the question, whether or not yours is a church of Christ, I submit again to your own decision.

Nor have you permitted a single leading doctrine of the Bible to escape your efforts to pervert them.

The Bible holds up one God as the sole object of religious worship. You teach us to worship the Virgin—the host—the cross; and to adore angels—departed saints—relics—and even pictures.

The Bible teaches that our only access to God is through a Redeemer, Jesus Christ, who is made unto us of God, wisdom and righteousness and sanctification, and redemption, and that through faith in his name we are made partakers of the blessings of his work of redemption. You teach that there are other intercessors to whom we must apply—that our own works are efficacious to save us—that the sacraments have inherent power to save—that faith in Christ is not the true method of justification.

The Bible teaches that we must be born again, created anew by the Holy Ghost. This you denounce as a false and accursed doctrine, and teach us that we are regenerated by baptism, and kept in a state of salvation by confirmation, confession, penance, fasts and alms.

The Bible plainly teaches that when we die we go to heaven or to hell, like Lazarus and the rich man, that our probation is confined to the present state. You teach us that there is a third state, Purgatory, where souls are purified from the stains of venial sins, and thus prepared for heaven. And so on to the end of the chapter.

Such, Reverend sir, is the way in which some things strike me, bearing on the question whether yours is, or is not, a church of Christ. That there are many papists truly pious, I believe. But whether a church fashioned as is yours, as to its external organization, after the Roman state when governed by military despots—departing, in its public worship, in every essential particular, from that taught in the Scriptures; whether a church which corrupts and suppresses the Bible—which corrupts its sacraments and its doctrines, is a church of Christ; this, this, is the grave question which I now submit to your decision. It is said that a question involving a vast amount of property was once submitted to Sir Matthew Hale. Before giving his opinion he was approached by the lordly defendant in the case with a bribe. He repulsed him with great indignation. His lordship complained of him to the king; and the reply of his majesty was: "Sir Matthew makes his decisions without fear or favour; he would treat me in the same way."

All I ask of you is to decide the above question with the honesty of Sir Matthew.

With great respect, yours,

KIRWAN

LETTER XI.

The effects of Popery on Liberty, Knowledge, Happiness, True religion.

My dear Sir,—In my last letter, I submitted to your decision the question, whether or not the Roman Catholic is a church of Christ, after briefly stating to you how some things bearing on its truthful decision strike me. I design the present letter to have no very remote bearing upon the same question; and would ask you to give it the degree of consideration to which, in candour, you may deem its statements entitled.

In reading the prophecies of the Old Testament, I find that they all speak with the most glowing anticipations of the yet future Kingdom of Messiah. That kingdom was to produce the civil, moral, and spiritual renovation of the world. When I turn over to the New Testament, I find that on the birth of Messiah, the Angel of the Lord stated to the shepherds that he came to bring them good tidings of great joy which should be to all people. And having announced the birth of the Saviour in the city of David, he was suddenly joined by a multitude of angels, singing, "Glory to God in the highest, and on earth peace, good will toward men." The Old Testament and the New,—patriarchs, prophets, and apostles, all unite in teaching us that the effect of Christianity upon our world would be to restore it to its primeval state, and to re-instamp upon the heart of man the lost image of his Creator. Now, how far has Popery fulfilled these predictions, and the reasonable expectations of the faithful, founded on them? In other words, what are the fruits of Popery? Our Saviour tells us that a good tree yields good fruit,—a bad tree, bad fruit. And with this test in view, my object in the present letter is to state to you how some things strike me.

What has been the effect of Popery upon *human liberty?* Permit me to use the word "liberty" in its widest sense. As to civil liberty, it has been its unchanging enemy. It has never permitted a spark of liberty to glow for an hour when it could extinguish it. There is not in Europe, at the present hour,—perhaps not on earth,—a greater civil despot than the Pope. The man that, in Italy, writes a page, or makes a speech in favour of liberty, must fly the kingdom, or be dragged to a dungeon. And we are to judge of Popery, not by its pliability where it cannot rule, but by the way which it shows its heart where it can do so without let or hinderance. Kings as well as people have groaned under its tyranny. Henry IV. of Germany was made by the Pope to stand three days in the open air, with bare head and feet. Frederic I. was made to hold his stirrup. He caused Henry II. of England to be scourged on the tomb of Thomas a-Becket. And the present state of Spain, Austria, Italy, show the effects of Popery on civil liberty.

It is equally the foe of mental liberty. The Bible is without any authority, save what your church gives it. And the Bible must teach nothing save what your church allows. And man must believe nothing save what the priest permits. And philosophy must teach nothing save what the church sanctions. You know that for this last offence Galileo was sent to study astronomy in prison. Pure popery and real liberty, never have breathed, and *never can*, the same atmosphere. The principle of your church is to allow nothing that bows not to its yoke.

What has been the effect of popery upon *human knowledge?* When Christianity like a new sun rose upon the world, there was much that might be called education in the Roman Empire. The obvious effect of Christianity was to extend it. After the lapse of some ages, popery by gradual stages crept, serpent-like, to the high places of power. How soon afterwards the lights of learning go out; how soon the dark ages commence, and roll on as if they were never to end! And those centuries of darkness form the golden age of your church. And what spirit did it manifest on the revival of learning in England after the sacking of Constantinople, and at the Reformation? Leo X. prohibited every book translated from the Greek and Hebrew. This blow was aimed at the Bible. He forbade the reading of every book published by the Reformers. He excommunicated all who read an heretical work. The Inquisitors prohibited every book published by sixty-two different printers; and all books printed by any printer who had ever published a book of heresy! Nor has one of these prohibitions been ever recalled. At this hour, the noblest products of human genius are under the ban of your church; and the Index Expurgatorius is in full operation at Rome!

And what has been the effect of all this upon human knowledge? Look into the countries, for an answer, where your church rules undisturbed. The nobles and the people, in Spain, Portugal, Austria, Sardinia, Sicily, are sunk into almost the same state of ignorance. Upon the intellectual degradation of Catholic Ireland I have already dwelt. The Book of books which the Lamb died to unseal, your church has re-sealed, ; it has laid an embargo upon human knowledge; it allows the people to read only what it permits; and it permits only what tends to rivet its chains, and to perpetuate the darkness which is its natural element. When the Reformation occurred, the retrograde movement of the world towards ignorance, and barbarism, and idolatry, had almost been completed. Had it not occurred, a radiance might continue to gild the high places of the earth after the gospel sun had set—a twilight might be protracted for a few ages, in which a few might grope their way to heaven—but each age would have come wrapped in a deeper, and yet deeper gloom, until impenetrable darkness had fallen on the world. Even the degree of knowledge which has obtained in the papal world, it owes to the Reformation.

And what has been the effect of popery upon the *happiness of our race?* This is a question of wide bearing, yet I can do little more than glance at it. Has it ever laid out its energies for the promotion of human happiness? If so, when and where? Has it not, on the other hand, set itself in opposition to every thing calculated to promote it? Does general intelligence promote it?—Your church has always opposed it. Does the free circulation of the Word of God promote it?—You have opposed this, also. Does the inculcation of pure religion promote it?—You have poisoned, or closed up all its fountains. Does advancing civilization promote it?—Your efforts are untiring to reverse its wheels and to roll us back to the darkness of the dark ages, whose very light was darkness. But what can I say more? for the time would fail me to tell of your monasteries and nunneries—of the wars which popery has excited—of its crusades—of the bitter jealousies it has sown between states—of the oceans of blood it has shed to obtain its objects—of the Inquisitions it has erected to torture the unbelieving—and of the way and manner in which it has caused those of whom the world was not worthy, to have trial of cruel mockings and scourgings; yea, moreover of bonds and imprisonment: how it caused them to be stoned, to be sawn asunder, to be slain with the sword; to wander about in deserts and in mountains, in dens and caves of the earth. O! Sir, the pathway of popery through the world is marked by the blood and bones of its victims. It has gone into the earth feeling that Joshua's commission on entering Canaan was in its pocket; and that all who questioned its authority were Hittites and Amorites. And almost without a figure of speech it can be said, that the nations which it found as the garden of the Lord, it converted into a howling wilderness. I know not that human happiness has ever had a more determined foe than popery.

What is the influence of popery as to the exercise of *Christian charity?* By charity I mean not almsgiving, nor yet the love of God which the Spirit inspires in the soul, but that grace which induces love to those who differ from us, and to cast a mantle over their defects. The Bible teaches us to do good to all as we find opportunity—to love our enemies—to treat with kindness those who despitefully persecute us. How does your church obey these injunctions of Christ the Lord? Let your inquisitions—your auto da fe's—your Bartholomew's day—your Irish massacre—your yearly anathemas against heretics—your consigning to perdition all beyond the pale of your church, answer. All non-papists you place beyond the pale of mercy—you refuse their bodies Christian burial, if such *your* burial can be called—you convert into the bitterest enemies of the man that becomes a Bible Christian, those of his own household—you make the poor Irish servant to feel that his master, and her mistress are the enemies of God, however pious, whose reading of the Bible, and whose prayers to heaven cannot be heard without committing great sin—you enact a ceremonia law, and proclaim that all who submit not to it are speckled with plague spots. And, hence, your priests, wherever located in Protestant communities, instead of going about, as men, to promote the general welfare, move about as spectres, as if afraid of the light of day; here abstracting a child from a Sunday school; there burning a Bible; here poisoning the mind of a servant against his master, and there that of a maid against her mistress;—and seeking to place all save his own unlettered followers, like the lepers of Samaria, without the city of God. Does this look like the spirit of Christ?

What is the influence of popery on *true religion?* To this point I have already spoken. I have told you, sir, how it has corrupted our Rule of Faith, and the sacraments, and the doctrines of the Bible. This is but the *theory* of the matter;—O, how can I speak of its practical effects? The religion of Christ it has converted into a system of idolatry in which God and witches—the Bible, and traditions, canons, decretals—the worship of God and of saints —the mediation of Christ and of Mary—prayer and scourging—pious deeds, penances and processions, are all of like authority, and like efficacy!

The mind of the poor papist it fills, not with light and love, but with darkness and fear. It closes to him the way to heaven through the blood of Christ, and opens it through the fires of purgatory. Leaving him in doubt as to where he will succeed best, he now prays for pardon to God—now to the Virgin now to Peter or Paul—now before some old picture almost obliterated by age—believing alike the truths of scripture, and the absurdities of your system, and knowing little of either.

It impresses the poor papist with the idea that religion consists, not in love to God and man, but in external submission to rites and forms. Hence, the Spaniard will go to confession with his dagger under his mantle—and the poor, generous Irishman, will go from the Mass and Missal to the pot-house. And your inquisitors have gone out from your eucharist to kindle the fires which consumed *your* heretics and *our* martyrs, and which illumined their pathway to glory!

But I must stop, lest my emotions swell beyond due bounds.

These, Rev. sir, are some, and but some of the fruits of your system. How do they appear to you when thus brought together? Is the tree which bears these fruits good, or bad? Has popery, in any one particular, in any one country, or in any age, ever produced the results which prophets and apostles have told us the religion of Messiah would produce? If not, are not popery and Christianity, not only different, but antagonist systems?

With great respect, yours,

KIRWAN.

LETTER XII.

Conclusion of the whole matter.

My dear Sir,—The letters which I have had the honour of addressing to you, I must now bring to a close. I have stated to you, with all frankness and sincerity, my reasons for leaving the church in which I was born, baptized, and confirmed; and which, on the most mature deliberation, yet prevent me from returning to it. I can assure you, on the word of an Irishman, and which is far more, on the word of a Christian, that I have had no end in view but the exposure of error, and the development of the truth. Thirty years have almost run their course since I left your church; and although not utterly unknown to the men of our age, nor unsolicited, these letters form my first appearance on popery. Unless some unexpected ripple is excited on the current of my feelings, they will, probably, form my last.

Now, dear sir, what think you of these reasons? Are they, or are they not, sufficient to excuse, to forbid my return to your church? Had I an ear sufficiently acute to hear the decision of your conscience, I believe in my soul that it pronounces them sufficient. Yes, I believe, that were it not for your sad doctrine of Infallibility, which stereotypes and perpetuates every absurdity, you and multitudes like you, men of sense and education, would rise and cast a fire-brand amid the rubbish which ignorance and wickedness have, in the progress of ages, collected around your church, and send its smoke heavenward like the smoke of a furnace. But, Sir, I am not ignorant of the slow progress of truth against bigotry—of the great difficulty of exchanging bad opinions and customs, hallowed by usage, for better ones. Nor have I read history so inattentively as not to learn from it the great difficulty of converting high ecclesiastics to the knowledge of the truth. The mitre has shielded many a head from the weapons of sense and logic; and under the surplice many a conscience has gone to rest that, without it, would have contended to the death for the faith once delivered to the saints. I must not forget that it was the high priest who occupied Moses' seat that put our Lord to death; nor can I forget that those claiming to be the successors of Peter, and the vicegerents of Christ, have been the greatest persecutors of the saints. They have shed Christian blood enough for pope and cardinals to swim in. Would to God that you could see things as I see them; your influence would be strong in freeing our fellow-countrymen from that bondage of the soul which most degrades them. But despairing of this, I turn from you to the victims of your system. Roman Catholics, and especially Irish Roman Catholics, to you I now turn. From your bishop, whom, with you, I respect as a man, though I oppose his religious principles, I appeal to you. With you is the power to bring to a perpetual end that system of ghostly tyranny the most oppressive that man has ever felt. Subjects and sceptres depart together; the farce of the Mass will soon end when there are none to witness it,—and popes, bishops, and priests will soon seek an honest calling when there are none to be edified by their jugglery,—when "the alms and the suffrages of the faithful" cease to flow.

Will you give an honest perusal to these letters; and candidly weigh the reasons and the arguments which they contain? That I was born in Ireland, is my pride. My sympathies are all with Ireland in its civil, social, and moral degradation. The blood of my kindred, shed to defend it against English oppression, mingles with its soil. Your present feelings as to your church, I have had, and in all their force. I can entirely appreciate them. I have cordially hated Protestantism and Protestants; and I have seen the time when I regarded the man as my personal enemy who would utter a word against my religion. But those were the days of my youth, and of my ignorance. When I became a man, I put away childish things. And my reasons for so doing are spread out before you in these letters; and all I ask of you is, kindly and candidly to consider them, and then to act accordingly. If they are not sufficiently cogent to cause you, as they have caused me, to leave the Church of Rome, then you will have my entire consent to be oppressed fleeced, and ridden by your priests, as long as you live.

Yet permit me to entreat you to give to the subject of these letters the attention which it demands. I know that many of you are sincere; but this is no test of truth. I know many of you to be devout; but so are Mahometans and pagans. I know that many of you are prepared to make any sacrifice which religion demands. But we may give all our goods to feed the poor, and our bodies to be burned, and yet be strangers to the only true religion. My heart is deeply affected in view of your state. A noble people, you are shut out from the joys to which God invites you. You are hoodwinked and manacled by a system of the grossest fraud and delusion; you are denied the common birthright of a citizen of the world—seeing with your own eyes and hearing with your own ears. You are robbed of the only volume that can guide you—and are forbidden to enter the way of life, save through the gate which is guarded by your priests. O! suffer the entreaties of one who suffered as you now do under the galling chains of papal tyranny. Break the fetters which priests have forged, and in which they have bound you. You are now in a land where you may laugh at the excommunications and anathemas of popes, prelates, and priests. God has given you his word; let no man filch it from you. God has given you a mind, to think for yourselves; let no man usurp the power of thinking for you. God invites you to himself, to receive at his own hand pardon and forgiveness. O! submit not to go and pay for these, and on your knees, to a priest. Go to the Bible for your religion. Receive nothing as religious truth, which is not there taught; and your mental, social, and moral regeneration is commenced.

But you meet this appeal with the objection, that I am a deserter from your church; and that I am not, therefore, to be heard. If your priests take any notice at all of these letters, I know well the changes they will ring upon this idea. But was not Peter a deserter from the Jewish church; and must he not be heard on that account? Must a man who renounces error never be heard by those who continue in it? And what think you of the persecution by your church of those who renounce its authority? To say the least of it, it is in bad company. The Jews put Christ to death for deserting the faith of Moses. The Mahometans put to death any man of their number who rejects the Koran for Christ. The Hindoos expel from their society all who reject their religion for ours. And popery has shed, in rivers, the blood of those who could not but reject its follies and absurdities. In this happy land, the bull of a pope is as harmless as a lamb—and the thunders of the Vatican have no lightning that injures. Priests may prejudice you against these letters, but they are the interested party,—their craft is in danger. And all I ask of you is, to give my reasons the candid consideration which you owe to yourself, and which their importance requires.

But you may ask, What! do you wish me to give up my religion? Is not mine the oldest religion? Here, I well know, is the invincible argument with many of you; but has it any weight? Are the oldest things always the best? If so, then the Jews were right in resisting Christianity; and the pagans are right in clinging to their false systems—and you do wrong in ever exchanging an old garment or an old house for a new one. But is popery the oldest religion? O, no; Christianity is older. Popery and Mahometanism arose at the same time, and centuries after the establishment of Christianity. They are alike corruptions of the religion of Jesus, though the prophet has apostatized farther than the pope. They both appeal to the senses, and are both idolatrous. If the pope has his holy water, the prophet has his holy well. If the one has his holy bones, and coats, and relics, the other has his holy pieces of tapestry from the temple of Mecca. They have alike their pilgrimages—their senseless repetition of prayers—their Lents—their penances, and their external symbols which alike adorn the church and the mosque. And if the papist can object to Christianity, saying, Is not mine the oldest religion? then can the Mahometan do the same.

But yours is not the oldest religion. I could here give you the time, did the limits of a letter permit, when the distinguishing doctrines of your church were introduced. The celibacy of the clergy came into the church in the Fourth Century; purgatory appeared in the Seventh, and was affirmed in the Twelfth; auricular confessions, and the worship of the Host, in the Thirteenth; and so on to the end of the chapter. And instead of wishing you to give up the oldest religion, we wish you only to give up popery for Christianity;—to give up the new, and to return to the old. All that I have done myself and all that I desire you to do is, to lay aside every thing that pope, bishops, and priests have added to the religion of Jesus, and to embrace that religion just as it is taught in the Bible.

Convinced that you have been deceived by those to whom you have been looking for guidance—that priests have sought your money more than your salvation—that instead of bread they have given you stones, and for eggs, serpents—that they have sought to brutalize, instead of enlightening you—to enslave instead of elevating you to the liberty with which Christ makes his people free; do any of you inquire as to the course best for you to pursue? If you will take the advice of one that has gone before you in the way, it is cheerfully given. Think not of giving up all religion because of the deceptions of popery. This was one of my mistakes. Take the Bible for your guide;—that will not deceive you. It teaches you that you are a sinner; this you should believe and feel. It teaches you that Christ died for sinners; and that his blood cleanses from all sin; and that to escape the wrath and curse of God due to you for sin, the great and the only prerequisites are repentance toward God, and faith in the Lord Jesus Christ. Give up your missal for the Bible—confess your sins not to your priests but to God—look for pardon and meetness for heaven, not to priestly ablutions, and eating wafers, and extreme unctions, but to the righteousness of Jesus Christ, received by faith; and in spite of popes, prelates, and priests, life, eternal life, is yours.

Wishing and praying for you all, that deliverance from popish thraldom in which I rejoice, and that gospel hope of future blessedness which is my stay and comfort in this vale of tears,

I am, with great respect, yours.

KIRWAN.

LETTERS

TO THE

RT REV. JOHN HUGHES,

ROMAN CATHOLIC BISHOP OF NEW YORK.

BY

"KIRWAN."

SECOND SERIES.

PHILADELPHIA:
PRESBYTERIAN BOARD OF PUBLICATION.

CONTENTS.

INTRODUCTION TO THE SECOND SERIES.

THE Letters in the New-York Observer addressed to Bishop Hughes, under the signature of "Kirwan," produced, as might have been expected, an extraordinary sensation. They were read, not by the Bishop only, nor by Protestants only, but by many in the bosom of the Church of Rome, who were thus led to see the absurdity of much which they had been taught to believe. One edition followed another in rapid succession: they were translated into the German language, and published for the thousands flocking to our shores and speaking that tongue: they were reprinted in England, and circulated among the Roman Catholics there and in Ireland, with what effect we have yet to learn.

But the Author, in assigning to Bishop Hughes the reasons that prevent his return to the church in which he was born, baptized, and confirmed, had by no means exhausted the catalogue, and he was repeatedly called upon to complete the work.

Of these calls, the following published in the Observer is a fair indication of the estimate in which the former series was held, and of the public desire that Kirwan would resume his pen.

To the author of the letters on Romanism, lately addressed to Bishop Hughes through the New York Observer, over the signature of Kirwan:

SIR,—Though you have chosen hitherto to keep in the shade in reference to the authorship of these letters, I suppose you are not buried in so deep obscurity as not to have some knowledge of what is passing in the world around you. But lest you should chance to be less knowing than might be presumed, I beg to state to you through your own channel of communication, that the letters to which I refer have been read by the religious community at large, with a degree of interest that has rarely been felt in reference to any similar publication. If I mistake not, the judgment of the world is that they are characterized by a simplicity and perspicuity that bring them fairly within the scope of any comprehension; by a force of thought and expression which no reflecting and impartial mind will find it easy to resist; by an amount of good nature and Christian charity which must prevent any reasonable opponent from taking offence; and last, though not least, by an unwonted pungency, which is likely, ere this, to have vibrated in a note of terror to the innermost heart of Rome. I believe, in common with a multitude of wiser and better men, that these letters have, as yet, only begun to fulfil their mission; and that those who live at the ends of the earth, and who are destined to live in coming years, will look upon them as having had much to do in lifting from the world one of its heaviest curses.

But my object in addressing you is something more than to inform you of that of which, I dare say, you need no information. You are aware that it is only a portion of the ground of the Romish controversy which your letters have occupied. There are many points of equal moment with those already discussed, which you have left untouched. Allow me to say, yours is the hand to sweep through this whole domain of error. It would be an occasion of deep regret if you should not carry forward to its completion a work which you have so happily begun. The Christian public expect, may I not say, demand it of you. The multitude who are yet in the same spiritual thraldom from which you have escaped, demand it. Your country, whose political as well as religious interests are threatened with deadly invasion, demands it. The cause of an enlightened Christianity, of a sound and evangelical Protestantism, demands it. There is a requisition upon you, KIRWAN, which I am sure you cannot resist without offending against the mercy that hath taken your own feet out of the miry clay, and established your goings. May the Head of the church enable you suitably to appreciate your obligations and responsibilities. Keep in the dark if you will: only lead others into the light of life and into the liberty wherewith Christ makes his disciples free. Be assured that in making these suggestions, I am

ONE OF MANY.

Obedient to these calls, and impelled by a sense of duty to his kinsmen according to the flesh, his countrymen and brethren, he has prepared this second series, in the same courteous and conciliatory style of the former: breathing the same national sympathy with Irishmen, and full of the humor that betrays the author's nativity, while it secures the attention of the reader.

Placed in the hands of those yet in the faith of Bishop Hughes, these letters will be read without prejudice, and followed, as I trust they will be, with the enlightening and convincing Spirit, they will work mightily in opening the eyes of those now wandering in error, and leading them to the knowledge of the truth.

SAMUEL IRENÆUS PRIME.

LETTERS

TO THE

RIGHT REV. JOHN HUGHES,

BISHOP OF NEW-YORK.

Second Series.

LETTER I.

Reasons for this Second Series—Why addressed to Bishop Hughes—Evil days have come upon Popery.

My dear Sir,—When I closed the letters I had the honour of addressing to you during the last spring, I fondly hoped that my part in the thickening controversy on Romanism in our country, had closed also. As those letters formed my first, I designed that they should also form my last appearance before the public on that topic. So I expressed myself to you in my closing letter. But the unexpected "ripple" has been "excited on the current of my feelings," and whether wise or otherwise, I have concluded again to address you.

My reasons for so doing, and thus departing from my original resolution, are briefly these: The public, who have so kindly received, and so widely circulated my 'Letters," have called for another series, embracing the reasons which I have omitted to state; and which, together with those stated, forbid my return to your church. At least one of the papers devoted to the interests of Popery in this country, calls upon me, in a semi-serious manner, to give my views on certain points which it raises, individuals of your communion, who have given my letters a candid perusal, have asked what Kirwan had to say upon this and that point not considered by me; and last, though not least, is a desire to put into the hands of every inquiring Roman Catholic, a complete manual of my objections to your church, candidly and kindly considered. These, Rev. Sir, are the reasons and motives, and not a love of controversy for its own sake, which induce me again to address you.

While yielding to these reasons and motives, I yet confess to you that I deem the present series of letters, which will be brief, a work of supererogation. If you have never performed such a work, you know what it means. My conviction is, that the reasons given in my former letters for refusing to return to your church, are sufficient; sufficient to induce any sane mind to withhold its faith from your teachings, and every sane man to abandon your church. This, you will say, is a partial decision; it may be so. But as a tree may be held in its place by a few weak roots after the main ligaments that bound it to the earth are cut, and when the weakest wind that blows may cause it to totter; so a mind, when the power of an ancient superstition over it is broken, may yet retain a connexion with it, influenced by reasons which seem unworthy of consideration. I know this to be the case. The belief in "witches and warls" was early impressed on the mind of Hume; and it is said of him, that, after he reasoned matter and mind out of existence, he could not hear the rustling of a leaf, after dark, without starting as if a witch were upon him. The taste and smell of a sour liquid remain long in the emptied cask. And if any mind, rejecting the great outlines of your system, is yet held to it by some reasons which I have not considered, and whose absurdity I may be able to expose, I feel anxious to relieve it. I must not withhold from you my deep conviction that Popery is an evil tree; that its fruits are only evil. I believe it to be a falling tree. Its branches are withering in the air, and the axe, wielded by an Almighty hand, is cutting its roots. And if I can assist in cutting a few more of its roots, and thus hastening its fall, I feel that I will be conferring a benefit upon our race, and contributing to the emancipation of millions of men from a slavery, in comparison with which that of the Pharoahs was freedom. Hence these additional letters. And all I intend doing, is to state to you some farther reasons which forbid my return to your church.

Before entering upon a statement of these reasons, permit me to say a few things which I can better say in this preliminary letter than any where else.

The question has, doubtless, suggested itself to your mind, and to the minds of others, why do I address these letters to you? Some of my reasons I have already given you. I believe you to be a man of sense, of learning, and of fair character, which cannot be said of all papal priests. You are put forth, now that Bishop England, also one of our countrymen, is no more, as the Achilles of your party in these United States. If any man in the country can refute my reasoning and obviate my objections, you can do it. And as my sole object and aim is the truth, I have selected the man, in my opinion, best fitted to correct me when in error; when false, to show me the fallacy of my reasoning,—and if he should reply, who would reply as a scholar and a gentleman. If you cannot confute me, no man of your church in these United States can. Nor will I consent to notice what may be said in the way of reply to, or abuse of these letters by any man, save yourself. I have, as they say, a drawing towards you as an Irishman—I respect your open and manly bearing, and, sadly as, in my opinion, you prostitute your talents, I have a high respect for them. Hence I pass through the ranks of soldiers, and by inferior officers, and go up to Achilles himself.

But you have not answered my former letters!

I confess to you, sir, that I had no expectation in writing them, that you would answer them, and for these reasons: First, because they are anonymous. And as I like not myself to contend with a masked opponent, so I judged of you. The text is capable of wide application, "as face answereth to face in water, so the heart of man to man." I prefer, for the present, to stand behind the curtain; and for this, among other reasons, that you and all men may decide upon what I say, simply upon the merits of my statements and arguments; and for the additional reason, to prevent a *personal* controversy. It is an old trick of your church to leave the argument for the man. And, secondly, because of their matter. I speak to you of what my eyes have seen; of what my ears have heard; of what my heart has felt. Facts are stubborn things. How can you make a man believe that to be sweet, which from actual taste he knows to be sour? It is hard to reason against a man's experience. On these grounds I expected from you no reply. And although, unless I mistake you, not one of the little men who seek to put the more abundant honour on the part that lacketh by a mock dignity, by an assumed superiority, yet you know when to be wisely silent. If, sir, without compromising your crosier,—*if*, during some hours of leisure from your varied and manifold duties, you would consent to answer some of the reasons and considerations which I have stated, and will state in the following letters, which forbid my return to your church, there is one, at least, that will read your reply with great pleasure. I am not, sir, among those who impute your silence to your inability to reply to my statements; but if I can only gain access to the public ear, if I can only obtain from candid Roman Catholics a careful consideration of what I say, your silence will give but little trouble. My object will be attained.

Permit me to make one other remark before closing this letter. Evil days have come upon the system of which you are so able an advocate. Once you could silence inquiry by church authority; but, in this country especially, that day has passed away. It is passing away even under the shadow of the dome of St. Peter's. There are those, yet, in this country and in the old countries of Europe, who, like that useless bird of sable wing, called the jackdaw, which you and I have seen in our youth, love the narrow window, and the toppling tower, and the mantling ivy, who hover about whatever is ancient, however worthless or truthless; but their number is small, and is daily diminishing. The great inquiry now is after the true, the scriptural, the reasonable. The day for the trial of all things has come. Mere authority in philosophy, in morals, in religion, is valueless. When man appeals from the Church to the Scriptures, it is of no avail to say to him, "believe the Church." No appeal is admitted from the Scriptures to the Fathers—from the teachings of Paul to the decisions of Councils. Old things, if absurd, are passing away; and their wrinkles only hasten their burial. Nor is there in the physical or moral sciences, nor in the science of government, nor in the theory of religion, a single principle that is not tried and sifted as if never tried before. At this treatment, hoary error may lift up its hands in holy horror, and fall back aghast as did Saul before the ghost of Samuel; but it cannot be helped. There may be, and doubtless is, a reckless speculation—a profane tampering with sacred things; but nothing will eventually suffer but the truthless. And what will become of Popery when proof and Scripture supplant authority and credulity?

It becomes you, then, sir, to buckle on the harness. The battle has but begun between truth and error. In your soul and in mine there should not be a desire but for the triumph of the truth. Let any opinion that I hold be proved unscriptural and unreasonable, and I will cheerfully give it to the hottest furnace you can heat to consume it. Let the truth of God triumph, whatever human systems perish. Will you join me in this aspiration?

In my next I shall proceed with my statement of some of the additional reasons which prevent me from returning to your church.

With grea respect, yours,

KIRWAN.

LETTER II.

Extreme Unction—Its meaning—The way of administering it—James v. 14, 15.—It enriches the Church—An Incident.

My dear Sir,—Agreeably to the promise made to you in closing my last letter, I now proceed to a statement of the additional reasons which yet prevent my return to the pale of your church, in which I was born, baptized, and confirmed. I shall begin with your sacrament of *Extreme Unction*. As but few of your own people, and yet fewer Protestants, understand it, I hope you and my readers will bear with me even if I should occupy this letter with its consideration. When rightly understood, it is a terrible sacrament. I will strive so to explain it as to bring it to the level of every mind, and from your own standard authors which lie before me.

The name of the sacrament explains it; it is anointing by holy oil of a sick person when recovery is *extremely* doubtful. This, and the fact that it is supposed to be the last act of religion, give it its name. The object of this anointing is thus explained by the doctors of Trent: "The devil is always busy in seeking to destroy the souls of men; yet it is at the hour of death that he most vehemently exerts all his power; and the object of this anointing by holy oil is to fortify the soul in the dying hour against the violent attacks of its spiritual enemies, and to enable it to make a holy death, and to secure a happy eternity."

The only person who can administer this sacrament is a bishop or priest. You admit a midwife, or a layman, to baptize; but a priest only can administer Extreme Unction. The reasons for this will appear in the sequel.

The oil used in this sacrament must not be common oil. That the effects intended may be produced, it must be oil of olives, "solemnly blessed by the bishop every year on Maunday-Thursday." I quote from Challoner; the sentence leaves it doubtful whether the efficacy of the bishop's blessing continues only a year, or whether the oil used must be blessed on that day. It has what is called in rhetoric, a squinting construction. As the bishop is paid for blessing it, it is probable he blesses but little at once, and that he gives it efficacy but for a limited time.

The effects and fruits of this anointing are these: it remits sins, at least such as are venial: it heals the soul of its infirmity and weakness; and helps to remove the debt of punishment due to past sins; it strengthens the soul to bear the illness of the body, and to repel its spiritual enemies; and "*if it be expedient for the good of the soul, it often restores the health of the body.*" I wish you, Sir, and my readers, to ponder the sentence in italics. Its meaning is this: if the person is restored, it is a miracle wrought by extreme unction; if he dies, restoration would not conduce to the health of his soul!!

The manner of administering this sacrament is as follows: If the time permits, certain prescribed prayers are said—the Confiteor is repeated, and absolution is granted—then the priest, making thrice the sign of the cross, says, "In the name of the Father, and of the Son, and of the Holy Ghost, may all the power of the devil be extinguished in thee, by the laying on of our hands, and the invocation of the holy angels, archangels," &c. Then dipping his thumb in the holy oil, he anoints the sick person in the form of a cross, upon the eyes, the ears, the nose, the mouth, the hands, and feet; at each anointing making use of this form of prayer: "Through this holy unction and his own most tender mercy, may the Lord pardon thee whatever sin thou hast committed by thy sight. Amen." And the same prayer is repeated, adapting the form to the several senses.

The requisite dispositions in the receiver are, faith in the sacrament—a pure desire for the health of his soul, and of his body if expedient—resignation—repentance—devotion.

In case of recovery and relapse, it may be repeated, and as often as the person relapses.

And your scriptural authority for all this you find in James v. 14, 15, which you thus translate: "Is any sick among you? Let him bring in the priests of the Church and let them pray over him, anointing him with oil in the name of the Lord; and the prayer of faith shall save the sick man, and the Lord will lift him up: and if he be in sin, his sins will be forgiven him."

Such is your Extreme Unction, as described by the Council of Trent, Challoner, and the Poor Man's Catechism. Although abridged, you, at least, will say that it is a perfectly fair abridgement. Let us now examine it in the light of Scripture and reason.

I ask you to look at your Greek Testament, and then to answer me on what authority you thus translate a portion of the 14th verse of James v.; "let him bring in *the priests* of the Church? Ah! the priests, the priests; this sacrament is for their benefit; and by a mis-translation, the power of anointing and praying must be confined to them!

But does the text afford the shadow of a support to the sacrament? No, not even the shadow. You utterly pervert the meaning of the apostle. The anointing and prayer of James is for the life of the sick; your anointing is for their death, and is never administered whilst there is any hope of life. The anointing of James is for the cure of the body;—yours is for the cure of the soul, in reference to which the text gives no direction. The saving of the sick, and the forgiveness of sins, are in consequence of the prayer of faith. Can none but a priest offer that prayer? The anointing of James and the prayers to be offered were to be followed with miraculous recovery; yours are to be followed with speedy death. The cures wrought by the anointing of James, were for the establishment of the claims of the Gospel;—yours, for the purpose of establishing the ghostly authority of your priesthood. That text above quoted is confessedly the only one on which you build your sacrament; and that text must be mistranslated, and utterly tortured out of its sense, and meaning, and end, even to afford a pretext to the use which you make of it. And this is but one of the many instances in which your church has changed and perverted the original meaning of the Scriptures, and forged them into chains to bind men to your system of delusion.

Having thus swept from your extreme unction the only scriptural authority claimed for it, and hung it up as a commandment of men, I have a few questions to ask in reference to it.

Is it so that God's people need the oil of olives, blessed on Maunday-Thursday, to be placed upon their eyes, and nose, and ears, and tongue, and hands, and feet, to secure the remission of their sins; and to heal the maladies of their souls, and to enable them to repel their spiritual enemies? If this oil can do it, what need is there of the blood of Christ? If the blood of Christ, and the presence of his Spirit can do it, what is the need of this olive oil?

But again; you require in the receiver of this sacrament, the dispositions stated above. Those are truly Christian dispositions, bating a few things in your manner of stating them. If these dispositions are possessed, will not the soul of the person be saved without your olive oil? If not possessed, will your olive oil save them?

Again; among the effects of this sacrament, as stated in the Poor Man's Catechism, p. 329, is this "it brings him (the sick man) in safety to the port of eternal happiness." Now, Sir, does extreme unction save from purgatory? This you will not say. If not, then it only takes him to *the port* of eternal happiness. From the port he is turned into purgatory. And your priests get paid for the olive oil by which he slips safely to the port of eternal happiness—and then they get paid for the masses by which they get him out of purgatorial fires into heaven! So that extreme unction is simply a device to increase "the alms and the suffrages of the faithful."

Again; what a low and sad view of the religion of God does this sacrament give to a dying man! It is administered to all that seek it on a dying bed. Let us suppose a case, which, no doubt, often occurs. There is a papist in the article of death. To this hour he has lived in sin. Feeling that death is upon him, he sends for his priest. He thinks now of nothing but confession—the eucharist, and extreme unction. The priest appears in his robes. If the sick man is able, he confesses. If not able, the anointing commences, and proceeds in the way already stated. He is crossed and anointed on his eyes, his nose, his tongue, his ears, his hands, and feet, and the prescribed prayers are said. The man now dies in peace, feeling that his sins are remitted—that his soul is healed of its infirmities—that his spiritual enemies are all subdued, through the efficacy of olive oil, blessed on Maunday-Thursday! Not a thought of the dying man is directed to the cross of Jesus Christ, or to the efficacy of his atonement! So that extreme unction is a papal incantation, by which the priest makes a deluded people to believe that the keys of heaven and hell hang by his girdle—that by his olive oil he can procure for them all that the Bible suspends on faith in Jesus Christ! Esteem me not harsh, Rev. Sir, when I declare it as my deep conviction, that by your sacrament of extreme unction, your church is deluding and damning multitudes of souls, and from year to year. It is a wicked substitution of olive oil for the blood of Christ at the dying hour, and simply and only for the benefit of your priests.

And what a tremendous use your church has made of it. Gaining access to the dying beds of kings, princes, and barons, in past days, with your olive oil, you have extorted millions of money from those who believed in your ghostly power. You have thus enriched the church and impoverished the people. You have built palaces for your bishops, and reduced the people to beggary. What will a dying sinner withhold from a man who, he believes, has the power to lock him up in hell; or by a little olive oil rubbed on with his thumb, can conduct him to the port of eternal happiness?

The man yet lives who narrates the following scene, of which he was an eye and ear witness. The chief of one of our Indian tribes, a man of great sagacity and decision, was on his dying bed. Many of his people, by a French Jesuit, were converted to the faith of your church. He knew the wiles of your missionary, and forbade him admission to his dying bed. The priest came with his olive oil, and pressed so hard for admission to him, that it was granted. "Stay," said the dying chief to the man who relates the story, "stay outside the door, and if I knock, come in." The priest entered, and the door was closed. Soon a violent knock is heard, and the man enters the room. "Take him out," said the dying chief; "take him out—land—land—give me land." The priest would put on the olive oil, but wanted first a grant of land.

Rev. Sir, your church must annul this sacrament of extreme unction, before I can return to its embrace. To my mind it is extreme nonsense. Should not incantations over dying men be left to Hottentots? I implore you to seek some other market for your olive oil, than the chambers of the dying.

With great respect, yours,

KIRWAN.

LETTER III.

PENANCE.

The pretended Sacrament described—No Scripture warrant for it—Its absurdities—A personal inquiry.

My Dear Sir:—With your leave, I will proceed with my statement of the reasons which prevent my return to the embraces of your church. Permit me to ask, in the present letter, your consideration of the reason which I deduce from your sacrament of *Penance*. It presents an objection as strong as your sacrament of Extreme Unction, which, without meaning to be irreverent, I have already pronounced Extreme Nonsense.

As but few, even of your own people, understand this sacrament, I will give a brief statement of it, and from your own authors.

Penance is a sacrament by which the sins committed after baptism are forgiven. Your doctrine is, that original sin is washed away in baptism; and that penance secures the forgiveness of all sins committed after baptism! Where is this distinction taught in the Bible?

On the part of the penitent, penance consists in contrition, confession, and satisfaction. Contrition is a hearty sorrow for sin, with a resolution to sin no more; confession is a full and sincere declaration of *all* our sins to a priest; satisfaction is a faithful performance of the prayers and good works enjoined by the confessor. So far for the penitent.

On the part of the priest, it consists in the absolution which he pronounces by the authority of Jesus Christ. The form of absolution is in these words: "I absolve thee from thy sins, in the name of the Father, and of the Son, and of the Holy Ghost."

The effects of this sacrament are thus stated in the "Poor Man's Catechism:" "It remits all the sins of the penitent without exception—restores him to the grace he had forfeited—replenishes his soul with the greatest peace, tranquillity, and spiritual delights, and reinstates him again in the friendship of God, as the prodigal son, after his return, was restored to his former honours in the house of his father." Wonderful results from such causes! May I ask here, if the parable of the prodigal son is meant to represent the way of return of a sinner to God, where did he stop to make confession and receive absolution?

None but a priest can grant absolution; and the power of the priest to absolve, you draw from John xx. 22, 23: "And when he had said this, he breathed on them, and said unto them, Receive ye the Holy Ghost. Whosesoever sins ye remit, they are remitted unto them; and whosesoever sins ye retain, they are retained," and from Matt. xvi. 15–19.

Such, Sir, in brief, is your sacrament of penance.

Let us now look at it in the light of Scripture and reason.

And let me first ask you, how do you make a sacrament of penance? Look at Chaloner's definition of a sacrament: "It is an outward sign or ceremony of Christ's institution, by which grace is given to the soul of the worthy receiver." Now, what is the outward sign of penance? It has no outward sign, no external ceremony. It is not a sacrament, according to your own rules. Your absolution is a different thing from your penance.

Again, two of the constituent elements of penance, confession and absolution, have no foundation in Scripture. Of confession I have already spoken. I have shown it to be a priestly device of the most fatal influence upon human liberty: its tendency to the corruption of morals is acknowledged. There is on my table a book, called "The Garden of the Soul," bearing on its title page your own name; and such a garden! Now, conceive yourself sitting in your confessional, and whispering through the little hole in its side, in the ears of a modest or immodest young girl of eighteen, or an amiable young wife of twenty-one years, the questions on pages 212 and 214! Sir, I dare not quote them here. I strove to read them to a friend a few days since, and before I got half through he cried out, "Stop, I can hear no more." The polluting confessional is a part of your sacrament of penance. Of absolution I shall speak in the sequel.

Look at the texts, for a moment, which you quote as teaching your power of absolution. It seems to me that if they were capable of any other interpretation than that which you give them, you would prefer it, in order to get rid of the monstrous power with which it clothes your priests. But alas! it is for the sake of that power that you pervert them. As there were various opinions entertained as to who Christ was, we hear him, in Matt. xvi. 15, asking his disciples, "Whom say ye that I am?" Peter replies, "Thou art Christ the Son of the living God." Jesus replies, "Upon this rock," that is, the confession of Peter that he was the Son of the living God, "I will build my Church." How simple and common sense!

Addressing Peter, and through him the other disciples, he says, "I will give thee the keys of the kingdom of heaven." Need I tell you, Sir, that by "the kingdom of heaven," here is meant the Church of Christ. Can such a master in Israel as you are be ignorant of this? This being so, "the keys of the kingdom" simply means, the power of admitting proper persons to the Church, and excluding improper persons from it. Keys, you know, were the ancient emblems of authority. How simple and common sense is all this.

Continuing to address Peter, and through him the other disciples, he says, "Whatsoever thou shalt bind on earth shall be bound in heaven; and whatsoever thou shalt loose on earth shall be loosed in heaven." To bind and to loose here are equivalent to bidding and forbidding, to granting and refusing, to declaring lawful or unlawful. The apostles were endued with the Holy Ghost, that they might infallibly declare the will of God to mankind, and determine what was, or was not, binding on the conscience—to show what persons ought, or ought not, to be admitted to the Church—and to decide on the characters of those whose sins were, or were not, forgiven. And whatever in these, or similar things, they bound or loosed on earth, would be bound or loosed in heaven. This is also the meaning of John xx. 22, 23, already quoted. This, Sir, I believe to be the common sense, the fair and just interpretation, of a passage on which your church has built up a priestly power, that has overshadowed the earth and enslaved nations. Where now, Sir, is your supremacy of Peter—your power of the keys—your power of absolution ? Gone, like the morning cloud before the sun. Blessed be God, you have not yet turned your keys upon the common sense of the world!

Now, Sir, look for a moment at some of the absurdities connected with your interpretations of the above texts. They are sufficiently startling.

Your church is built upon Peter. " Thou art Peter, and upon this rock I build my church." So that your church is built upon the *person* of Peter; ours is built upon the truth declared by Peter. Is, Sir, your rock as our rock ?

Is your church built upon Peter? Now turn from the 19th verse of the 18th of Matthew, which we have been considering, to the 22d and 23d verses of the same chapter. Peter is represented as rebuking his Lord, for the intimations he had given of his approaching death. But the Master, turning upon Peter, thus addressed him: "Get thee behind me, Satan." So that, on your principles of interpretation, your church must be built upon Satan!

What your priests, however profane or wicked, bind or loose upon earth, is bound or loosed in heaven. Now, here is a wicked man absolved by a priest; does he go to heaven? Here is a good man bound by a priest; does he go to hell? It must be so, on your principles. But you say he must be a sincere penitent, to gain any benefit from absolution. But if truly contrite, he can get to heaven without your absolution.

Take another case: the man bound by the curate may be loosed by the parish priest. I take the following illustration from a book before me: A penitent is enjoined to abstain from breakfast every morning, until his next confession. Christmas day intervenes, and he eats breakfast; not thinking that that day could be included. On confessing this at his next confession, the curate drove him from his knee, declaring that he would have no more to do with a person that so trifled with his commands. On the borders of despair, he went to the parish priest, telling him the whole story. "Do not mind it, my child," said the kind-hearted father, "I will confess you." He did so, and absolved him. Here one priest binds sin on his soul, and another unbinds it. He dies in this state. What becomes of him? Does the binding of the curate send him to hell, or does the loosing of the parish priest send him to heaven? What becomes of him? Is he suspended somewhere between heaven and hell?

But let us look at the *satisfaction*, which is a part of the sacrament of penance. "It consists in a faithful performance of the penance enjoined by the priest to whom we confess, whether as to restitution, or prayers, or alms-deeds, or fasting, to make some reparation, by these eminent good works, for the injury done to God." The penance enjoined by the priest is an "exchange which God makes of eternal punishment which we have deserved by sin, into these small penitential works." I quote from Chaloner. And without satisfaction like this, the sinner cannot be saved.

Now, Sir, will you tell me where this is taught in the Scriptures? Where are we told tha the blood of Christ is not sufficient to cleanse from all sin? Where is authority given to ministers or priests to exchange "eternal punishment for small penitential works?" Where does the Bible make a difference between ante-baptism and post-baptism sins?

Take another view of this thing. Penance means punishment. And "prayers, fasting, and alms," are enjoined by the priests as penance; that is, as punishment. So that your church makes prayers a punishment to atone for sins! What the Bible makes a privilege, you make a punishment! The fasting which is beneficial, is that to which we are led by a sense of our sins: you enjoin it as a punishment! And can alms-giving be a punishment, save to the worshipper of money? What are the prayers or alms worth that are offered or given as a punishment?

The penance enjoined, and the austerities voluntarily practised, are sometimes very singular, when considered in the light of making atonement for sins. Sometimes they consist in a set number of "Our Fathers" and "Hail Marys," counted on the beads or fingers, once or oftener a day, for so many days; sometimes in fasting for a given time, on given days, from meat, eggs, &c.; sometimes in a short pilgrimage to St. John's well, or St. Patrick's; sometimes, in Ireland, in going to the Seven Stations, and walking on bare knees on the ground from one station to another. The penances enjoined by the priest are optional and multiform, and are modified according to his own prejudices and the dignity of the confessing penitent. Some of the voluntary austerities are curious enough. St. Dominick, when a child, would leave his cradle and lie upon the cold ground. I have seen many an urchin do this whose name is not yet, and is not likely to be, in the calendar. St. Francis used to call his body, Brother Ass, and whip it as badly as Balaam did his. St. Francis Loyola put on iron chains and a hair shirt, and flogged himself thrice a day. He deserved it all. St. Macarius went naked six months in a desert, suffering himself to be stung with flies, to atone for the sin of having killed a flea. Now, is it not a wicked burlesque upon the religion of God, to make ignorant people believe that in these and similar ways they secure an exchange of eternal punishment? Language supplies no words in which I can express to you my deep abhorrence of your sacrament of penance.

Picture to yourself, Rev. Sir, this whole thing. There is a papist who has sinned grievously after baptism. How can he get to heaven? Through the sacrament of penance. It is not sufficient that he repent of it; no, he must confess to you; then he must perform all the austerities that you enjoin; then you absolve him; and then, taking up the key that hangs by your girdle, you open to him the kingdom of heaven. So, then, it is in your power to say who shall and who shall not enter heaven. What blasphemous assumption, when the divine Saviour tells me, and proclaims to all men, that "he that believeth on the Son hath life." Such assumptions are only worthy of the world's scorn.

It is amazing how men, pretending to be religious, could contrive such a sacrament. It is amazing how rational men can believe it. But it is not amazing how men believing it, and in the power with which it clothes you, should fawn at your feet as spaniels. It is no wonder that they pour their treasures into your coffers as water.

I believe in repentance, and hope I am not a stranger to it. I reject penance, as a priestly device to rob the people of their money and ruin their souls. Your church must lay aside this terrible sacrament before I return to her embrace.

Before closing, let me ask you one question. Do you believe that none go to heaven from New-York but those to whom you and your priests, with your keys, open its gates? It takes a hard heart and a soft head to believe this. I charge you with neither

With great respect, yours,

KIRWAN.

LETTER IV.

Miracles—Milner's vindication—Many examples—Legends of the saints—A miracle of my own working—Why so few miracles since the Reformation.

My Dear Sir:—Another reason which prevents my return to the bosom of your church, I draw from the *miraculous power* claimed for your saints and clergy. I have felt disposed to say nothing on this subject, because of the extravagance of the claim itself; and because of my reluctance to state the absurdities which crowd the legends of your saints, and which your church has palmed, and yet palms on the world as miracles. I feel afraid that some candid papist will conclude that I have at last commenced drawing on my imagination, and that the influence of my former reasoning with him will be weakened, by the utter, the intense absurdity of the miracles claimed for your saints, which I shall quote. But, pledging myself to fairness of statement, I will risk the consequences.

Milner, as you know, devotes his 23d letter to vindicate the possession of this power by your church. He says, "the Catholic Church being always the beloved spouse of Christ, and continuing at all times to bring forth children of heroic sanctity, God fails not in this, any more than in past ages, to illustrate ner and them by unquestionable miracles: accordingly, in those processes which are constantly going on at the apostolical see, for the canonization of new saints, fresh miracles of a recent date continue to be proved, with the highest degree of evidence, as I can testify, from having perused, on the spot, the official printed account of some of them." And miraculous power is claimed by all your writers, and is put forth as an evidence of yours being the true church; and its absence from Protestant churches is considered by you a conclusive evidence against them.

Milner not only claims this power for your church, but gives the following miracles that were performed, to his own certain knowledge and belief: Twenty years before it happened, a nun predicted the fate of the king and queen of France, Louis XVI. and his consort, who were beheaded. In 1814, Joseph Lamb fell from a hay-rick and injured his spine. At Garswood, in England, is preserved the hand of one Arrowsmith, a priest, who was put to death at Lancaster, in the reign of Charles I. Lamb was signed on the back by this hand, with the sign of the cross, and was instantly healed! In 1809, Mary Wood, in striving to open a window, greatly injured her arm, so as almost to lose the use of it. She employed physicians in vain. She finally had recourse to God, through St. Winfred, by a *Novena*—that is, prayers offered for nine days. She put a piece of moss from the Sain 's well on her arm, and it was instantly restored! Miss Winifred White, for some time diseased with a curvature of the spine, was healed in an instant of time, by bathing in Holywell! Milner was not a witness of any of these miracles; but they were proved true to his satisfaction! Marvellous marvels!

Now, Sir, permit me to add to these miracles a ew others from the Legends of the Saints, and no doubt equally well attested as those adduced by the learned Milner. As I have but few of these legends before me, I will quote from a recent review of the "Lives of the English Saints," now in a course of publication by those marvellous men, the Oxford divines, worthy of a place in the museum as Protestant curiosities.

Somewhere near York, St. Augustine restored a blind man to his sight. St. Sulpicius, when a mere child, drove away, with the sign of the cross, two black demons who strove to scare him from his devotions. St. Amatus miraculously stopped a lofty rock in the midst of its descent, with which a fiend sought to crush him in his cell. The father of St. Furceus contracted a clandestine marriage with a king's daughter. When the king found that she was likely to be a mother, he ordered her to be burned. She shed such a flood of tears as to put out the fire. Finding he could not burn, he banished her, and Furceus was born in a foreign land. St. Mochua had to call the stags from the forest to feed the multitude of his followers. He ordered their picked bones to be placed in their skins, and by an incantation over the skins and bones the stags were brought to life, jumped up, and ran back to the woods. St. Euchadius did the same with an old favorite crow, that he had to kill to provide meat for his guests. The piety of St. Fechin was so fervent, that when he bathed himself in cold water the water became almost boiling hot. When St. Mochua wanted a fire in his cell, he called down a fire from heaven to light it. St. Goar of Treves, wanting a beam to hang up his cape, hung it on a sunbeam, where it remained until he took it down. St. Columbanus miraculously kept the grubs from his cabbage. When St. Mael was in want of fishes, he caught them on dry ground; and St. Berach, when in want of fruit, made willows to bear apples. St. Fechin, when hungry, turned acorns into pork. In travelling he was stopped by a large tree which fell across his road: he commanded it to make way, and it instantly rose to its place. He built a mill on a hill top: being asked about the water, he went to a lake, a mile distant, into which he threw his stick; the stick followed him on his return, and the water after it, and the mill worked finely. Some thievish crows carried away some of the thatch of St. Cuthbert's hut to build their nests: at his rebuke they not only made an apology, but they brought him a piece of hog's lard to make amends for the injury. To this miracle Bede testifies. A raven plucked out the eye of an ass of St. James of Tarentaise: the saint made a hasty invocation, and the raven immediately returned and put the eye in its place, without the least injury to the ass. St. Augustine was treated with insults in a certain town in England—the fishmongers being especially active in the bad work, hanging the tails of fish upon his garments and those of his followers. For generations afterwards the children of that place were born with tails.

Your legends narrate miracles like these to any amount; and they are now reproduced from the French and English press, for the purpose of encouraging the faith of the pious. Wonderful as these are, they are by no means as wonderful as many others that the limits of a letter forbid me to quote.

And some of the saints wrought a profusion of miracles. St. Fechin was a wonderful hand at them. St. Francis far surpassed the Saviour himself. Christ was transfigured but once—St. Francis more than twenty times. St. Francis and his disciples restored more than a thousand blind to sight—and more than a thousand lame to the use of their limbs—and more than a thousand dead to life!

Now, sir, whilst these things are gravely narrated in your legends, and are read by your common people from your own books with the most pious belief in their truth, it is more than probable that this statement of them will be denounced as a bundle of Protestant lies! When a boy I read a life of St. Francis Xavier, which narrated miracles wrought by him far surpassing any here cited.

But why go to the miracles of the legends; you

are daily performing miracles which come up to any of them. Your daily changing of a wafer into the real body of Christ, and then eating him, beats any thing St. Fechin ever did. Your preparing an old sinner for heaven by rubbing him with olive oil, and then opening its gates to him by the keys which are only in your possession, far surpasses Fechin's turning acorns to pork. We believe the swine themselves are constantly doing this in our western woods. And in Ireland your priests are constantly performing miraculous cures on men and cattle. Even your common people there work miracles. When a thunder storm is raging, they kindle a fire, and heat the tongs red hot. This preserves their cattle from the lightning. If they are killed notwithstanding, it is in chastisement for some sins not confessed, or some penances not rightly performed. Perhaps, Sir, it may astonish you when I tell you that I myself, whilst yet in your faith, wrought two or three. Near my father's residence was a wood in which a man was once killed. His ghost was regularly seen after dark. I never passed through that wood without crossing myself, and saying Hail Mary. And I assure you I never saw the ghost. After dusk, in the spring of the year, I was sent on an errand to a neighbor's house, which was separated from ours by two or three fields. As I ran along I saw through the magnifying twilight what was obviously an evil spirit. I stopped suddenly, and the sweat commenced pouring. Naturally of a resolute spirit, I thus reasoned: if I run back he can catch me; if I go forward he can but catch me. So after saying my Hail Mary, and crossing myself, I went forward with a trembling step. As I advanced the horns of the fiend became perfectly obvious. Almost dead with fear I rushed forward and caught hold of them. And marvellous to narrate, those fiendish horns were instantly turned into the handles of a plough! Now I submit it to you, sir, whether these miracles wrought by myself, are not as great as those wrought by St. Mochua, or St. Columbanus. And yet I fear my chance for canonization is exceedingly small.

But considering the grave effects which have followed this claim of yours, it ought not, perhaps, to be treated lightly. And yet it is difficult to treat it otherwise.

Now, sir, will you say that the miracles adduced by Milner are worthy of a moment's consideration? Look at them again. A man hurt his back by falling from a hay-rick, and is cured by a dead man's hand! A girl in opening a window cut her arm, and felt difficulty in using it; she puts on a piece of moss and her arm gets well. Another girl has a diseased spine; she is cured by bathing in Holywell. Are these proofs to any mind that your church possesses miraculous power? If these are not, can the miracles selected from the legends of the middle ages be?

Can you, for a moment, place any of your miracles on an equality with those wrought by the Saviour and his apostles? Milner does it, sad I am to say, but will you, John Hughes, do it, and in the city of New-York? What! place these marvels of lying legends, the productions of infamous monks of the dark ages, who made saints of necromancers, and miracles of witch stories, on the same foundation as the miracles of Christ! Will you gravelv tell us, that if we deny the one we must deny the other? If I deny that the fervor of the piety of St. Fechin almost made the cold water to boil in which he bathed, must I also deny that Christ raised Lazarus from the grave? Will you, claiming to be a bishop in the church of God, say that these miracles are sustained by evidence equally conclusive as those of the Scriptures? This I will only believe when you say so.

Compare the object of scriptural and popish miracles. The cne are divine attestations to the truth; the other, to yours being the true church. How different these objects! And they are no more different than the miracles. And in point of force and evidence, Milner's miracles cannot be compared to those of Irving, or of our own Mormons.

If your church possesses miraculous power, why so sparing of its use since the Reformation? If they are not all impostures, why so many in Ireland, whilst tnere are none in Scotland; why so many in France and Spain, and so few in New-York? Come out in the open view of some intelligent Protestants, and cure a man that was born blind, or raise one from the grave that lay there until putrefaction commenced, and, then, we will ask you to excuse the utter scorn with which, until then, we must treat your impostures. My dear Sir, the world will not forget the history of Hohenlohe, the modern St. Fechin. He was forbidden to work his miracles save in the presence of some commissioners and physicians; he appealed to the pope. The holy father enjoined him to conform. From that hour his miracles have ceased.

"Ghosts prudently withdraw at peep of day."

Miracles were vouchsafed by God divinely to attest the truth of the Gospel. This power was vouchsafed to the Apostles, and was continued in the church until the truth of the Gospel was established. Then it was withdrawn. Since the rise of popery there has been no miracle wrought. The nearest approach to one, that I now remember, for fourteen hundred years, is the fact that your church could gain such a general credence for its absurdities, and make men believe that she could work miracles.

You must give up your lying legends and your claim to miraculous power, before I can return to your fold. I feel as did our fellow-countryman with the bad asthma, who exclaimed, "If once I can get this troublesome breath out of my body, I'll take good care it shall never get in again."

With great respect, yours,

KIRWAN.

LETTER V.

Marks of the Papal being the true Church considered. Unity—Sanctity—Catholicity—Apostolicity—Infallibility.

Rev. and dear Sir,—In the present letter, I wish to place before you another of my reasons for not returning to the church of my fathers, drawn from *the exclusive claims of your church*—claims which, if well-founded, consign to eternal damnation all who refuse to believe its doctrines, or to submit to its authority. That these claims are put forth, you will not deny. You glory in them. Milner and Butler assert them, and seek to sustain them by Scripture and reason. "The Poor Man's Catechism," from which I like to quote, because it is the channel through which you seek to impress the common mind, says, "those who submit not to the doctrine and authority of the Holy Catholic Church, are all out of her communion; as pagans, infidels, Turks, Jews, heretics and schismatics." And by the Holy Catholic Church is meant, that church whose head is the pope. This is sufficiently explicit. So that in your estimation, and in that of your church, the Protestant churches around you are no better than Jewish synagogues, or pagan temples; the people that worship in them, are no better than

Turks or pagans; and such men as the late excellent Milnor, as Spring, Knox, Bangs, Williams, Wainright, Skinner, your cotemporaries, and equals, and fellow citizens, are no better than Hume, Voltaire, Gibbon; or at least, than Jewish Rabbies, Turkish Mufties, or Hindoo Priests, who mingle their blood with their sacrifices. That such is your belief is apparent in your conduct. You and your priests so treat them. The belief of your people is, that all beyond the pale of your church are devoted to destruction. I remember the day when I had no more doubt of it than of my own existence. If there are papists who believe otherwise, and who exercise a charitable hope as to the salvation of Protestants, as I believe there are many, so far forth they are not papists.

The process by which you reach this terrible dogma is a very short one. There is no salvation out of the true church—the Roman Catholic is the true church—therefore, there is no salvation out of the Roman Catholic Church. Here is your logical and theological guillotine, by which you sever the hopes which bind millions of your race to God and heaven; who serve the one, and deserve the other, at least, as well as you do. And, then, the marks of yours being the true church, you parade before us with as much confidence as if they were true; and with as much assurance as if they were never, instead of being a thousand times, refuted. Permit me, in the briefest manner, to consider each of these marks. They are Unity, Sanctity, Catholicity, Apostolicity, and Infallibility.

Your first mark is *Unity*. Has your church this mark? In what one thing are you united? Not in the head of the church. You have a pope;—some say, others deny, that he is the head. One goes for the pope,—another for a general council,—a third for both united. Is this unity? But if we admit your unity, what follows? Does the agreement of numbers in maintaining error and superstition, prove that in which they are united true? Then Paganism, and Mahometanism, and Budhism, may be proved divine. These systems have more followers than you can boast.

You are not agreed as to the authoritative councils of your church. You are yet agitated by controversies on the subject. Nor are you agreed in the doctrines of the Bible. Never were Arminians and Calvinists more widely separated on these matters than you are. Look at the fierce contentions of your Jansenists and Jesuits, unsettled to the present hour. If united, what meant the fierce controversies of your Scotists and Thomists—of your Canonists and Schoolmen—of your Nominalists and Realists. But I cannot weary you or my readers on this matter. You talk about the differences among Protestants;—they are not to be compared to those among papists. You put into my hand Bossuet's "Variations of Protestants;" I put into yours,

"Edgar's Variations of Popery." Where Protestants differ in one point, papists differ in five,—where they differ in minor matters, you differ in the veriest essentials. Protestants agree as to the Head of the church, Christ;—and as to the rule of the church, the Bible. You differ as to both.

True, you have an apparent external unity. But how have you gotten it? What is it worth? You set up monstrous claims, and all who do not admit them you cast off. Milner's "Apostolical Tree," shows how the work of lopping off has progressed. You have laid the axe upon every green and fruitful branch; and the old stump and withered branches remain, a unity! And what is your unity worth? If I return to your church, "I must believe whatever the Holy Catholic Church believes and teaches." This I must do without knowing, and without ever being able to know, *all* that she believes and teaches. I must put myself into your hands, and give you power to think for me, and to believe for me; and then I must believe, and swear to, what you thus think and believe for me, at the peril of being cut off and cast into the fire. Sir, this is horrible slavery. Do you think men will long submit to it?

Your boasted unity is a fable—your apparent unity, is slavery. You present a united front in your opposition to Protestants; but never were the bowels of the victim of the Asiatic cholera more terribly convulsed, than is the bosom of your church by distracting controversies. Your priests and bishops and people may fight as they may, but they are a unity as long as they remain within the same organization. If one of them secedes, if you cannot kill him, you damn him, for the sake of unity.

Your next mark is *Sanctity*. I admit that sanctity, or holiness, is a mark of a true disciple, and of a true church. The people and church of Christ should be holy in all manner of conversation. Sanctity you claim for your church as one of its distinguishing marks. But in what is it manifested? You reply, first, in her doctrines. But what doctrine of the Bible has not your church corrupted? What institution has it not perverted? And so conscious is your church of this, that it withholds the unadulterated word from the people. You reply, again, *in the means of holiness.* By these you mean *the sacraments.* But you have grievously perverted the only two sacraments instituted by Christ; and you have added to them five which have no divine authority, and whose only object is to give you power, and to obtain for you "the alms and the suffrages of the faithful." You reply again, *in her fruits of holiness.* By these you mean the virtues practised by papists. I could not, for a moment, deny the true piety of many papists, the exalted piety of some; but will you, Sir, assert that the piety and virtues of your people are so much more resplendent than those of any, or all other people, as to mark yours as the true church? If so, it seems to me that you would assert that Jupiter surpasses the moon, and the moon the sun, in brightness. The evidences to the contrary are no more apparent in the one case than in the other. Look at the mass of your clergy in the sunniest days of your church, and what were their fruits of holiness? Your own historians being witnesses, what were the fruits of your nunneries, your monasteries, your monks, and your other orders, when there were no Protestants to unveil their enormities? What are now the fruits of your religion in the states of South America? Have you seen the testimony of Mr. Thompson, our late minister to Mexico, as to the papal clergy of that country? As to the fruits of holiness, compare Spain, Italy, with Scotland or New England.

But I will not proceed with the comparison farther than to ask you to compare the Protestant ministry of New-York with the papal—the congregation of St. Patrick's with any large and wealthy Protestant congregation in the city, as to the fruits of holiness, and you yourself will be astonished at the difference. The general rule is, that purely papal countries are those most debased and immoral, and purely Protestant countries are those most enlightened, and most abounding in every good work. The tenth century, the noonday of popery, was the midnight of our race. Nor does the history of the world present such evidences of unbridled, overgrown depravity, as does the history of your church.

Your next mark is *Catholicity*. You claim this

title for your church as to time, persons, and places. As to time, your church rose upon the ruins of that founded by Christ and his apostles, and centuries after their death. The peculiar doctrines and ceremonies of popery are derived from the heathen, and were engrafted on Christianity. Instead of your church, as you claim, being identical with that of Christ and his apostles, there is not an essential particular, in which it is not in opposition to it. I admit, as to persons, that yours is a very numerous church; but it never formed a third part of Christendom. Is the standard of truth the numbers that profess it? Then Christianity was a lie whilst in the minority;—and so it is a lie yet, because, taking our whole race together, vastly in the minority. So I admit, as to places, that popery is very widely diffused. But is not Protestantism also? Where has a papist gained foothold where there is not a Protestant? So that your claim to this mark is as absurd as it is groundless. Your catholicity is a vain and empty boast. There is a Catholic Church, but it is not yours.

Your next mark is *Apostolicity*—that is, a regular succession from the Apostles in the chair of St. Peter. Now, Sir, this claim is put forth by other churches as strongly as yours, and on foundations even stronger than yours. I now refer to the Armenian, Nestorian, and Syriac churches, which were founded before the Gospel was preached at Rome. It is beyond the power of man to establish this claim. If established, must we receive as a true minister every man coming to us in the regular line, whatever be his doctrines or morals? What is the test of apostolicity? Is it succession, or doctrines? Most obviously doctrines. "If there come any unto you, and bring not *this doctrine*, receive him not into your house, neither bid him God speed." Standing upon this one text, I would turn you away from my door, even had I seen the hands of all the apostles upon your head, unless you preached their doctrines. Why, the strong language of Paul would even warrant me to curse you, coming to me with your claim of succession, without apostolical doctrine. Read it:—"But though *we*, or an *angel from heaven*, preach any other Gospel unto you, than that we have preached, let him be accursed." Sir, if I try your succession by your doctrine, the true test of succession, I could soon place you among those who said they were apostles and were not. From what Apostle, save Judas, many are descended, who are crying out, Apostolical succession, apostolical succession! I cannot conceive.

Your next mark is *Infallibility*. Under all the circumstances of the case, this claim is truly ludicrous. Where is the seat of infallibility? Some say it resides in the pope. But how is he made infallible? The pope dies; an election for a new one is ordered. He is to be elected from the cardinals—all fallible men, if no worse. After endless intrigue, and boundless corruption, and numerous ballotings, the lot falls upon a fallible cardinal. Will you tell me how such an election makes him infallible? But others say, that the pope is not infallible, and that he may be deposed for heresy. So that here you are divided.

Some say the seat of infallibility is a general council. But how is this? Here are three hundred fallible men assembled in general council; how do they become infallible? Will you tell me the process? How do finites make an infinite? Heap them up as you may, are they not a heap of finites? And crowd together as many fallible men as you may, are they any thing else than a crowd of fallibles? But by what chemical or alchemical process can you deduce the infallible from the fal lible?

Nor is this the worst. We find one general council denouncing another—the church of one age contradicting the church of another. The seat of infallibility is thus undetermined by you; whilst the proofs of your church's fallibility fill the world. It is infallibly certain that your church is fallible.

Thus is your church, utterly destitute of every mark of being the true church, which you claim for it. Its unity is discord, or slavery—its sanctity is corruption—its catholicity is assumption—its apostolicity and infallibility each a lie. Could I speak of your church in the masculine and feminine gender, as do some of your writers, instead of admitting her to be the one, holy, catholic, apostolical, and infallible church, I would call her the mother of harlots, and the father of lies; the man of sin fully revealed, with "powers, and signs, and lying wonders."

And yet, whilst common sense rejects your claims, and common reason disproves them, and the Bible denies them, unless in the case of invincible ignorance, you cut off all beyond your pale from all communion with God—from all hope of heaven! I regard this as simply wicked. To gain your point, you rob the Father of us all of his goodness; man you drive to despair, and you convert God into a tyrant. If a boat were as rotten as I believe your church to be, I would not trust it to carry me across the North river. And yet it claims the entire monopoly of carrying to heaven all the souls that ever enter it, and for no reason, human or divine, that I can see, unless it be for the freight.

My Bible tells me, Sir, that whosoever believeth in the Lord Jesus Christ shall be saved. The sincere believers in the Lord Jesus Christ, whether in your church or other churches, or in no church, form a part of that church which Christ will present to the Father, without spot or wrinkle or any such thing. By setting up its claim to be the only true church—by denying salvation to all but your own members, with the exception of the invincibly ignorant, you deny this doctrine of the Bible and of my faith—you lay down a principle, unsustained by sense or Scripture, from which the mind of the world revolts, and from which my soul turns away, as from a thing the most offensive. Your exclusive claims must be proved, or abandoned, from their Alpha to their Omega, before I can return to your church.

With great respect, yours,

KIRWAN.

LETTER VI.

Relics—Relics the parent of miracles—The importance of relics—Specimens of relics—The abuses of relics—Indulgence—To whom and by whom granted—Their fearful effects

REV. AND DEAR SIR:—Permit me to ask your kind attention, in the present letter, to two more objections which prevent my return to your church, drawn from *your use of relics* and *indulgences.* The importance which you attach to these things, and the evils which flow from them, demand a letter for the due consideration of each; but I will consider them both in one, and, as I trust, without weakening the force of my objections.

"Relics are the dead bodies or bones of saints, and *whatever belonged to them in their mortal life.*" The clause I place in italics enables you to multiply them indefinitely. These relics are honored with an inferior and relative, but not with divine honor. And they are honored, 1st, because they were the temples of God; 2dly, because they are to be raised from the dead; 3dly, because of their miraculous power; 4thly, because they encourage the faithful to imitate their virtues. This is Challoner's account of them, with which that of Milner agrees.

This doctrine of relics is intimately connected with that of miracles—it flows from it. The man who performed miracles, when living, should be, after death, highly honored; his bones may perform them after death; and, as in many cases they do perform them, their relics should be honored with an inferior and relative, but not with a divine honor. Here is the link which connects your doctrine of relics with your miracles.

Relics are matters of immense importance to Rome. They are to your churches what the ark of the covenant, and the pot of manna, and Aaron's rod that budded, were to the Jewish temple. Hence the prodigious efforts of past ages to obtain relics, and the enormous prices paid for them, in order to place them in churches, and the sleepless vigilance with which they have been guarded, lest they should be stolen for the adorning of new churches by their virtues. They have been more than mines of wealth to Holy Mother, as they have brought her the gold and the silver, without the trouble of mining, smelting, or coining it.

If a bone or a relic of a saint could be secured for a new church, the church was called by his name, and placed under his guardianship. This is the origin of calling churches after the names of saints. And thus nations were placed under the guardianship of saints—as Ireland under that of St. Patrick—Scotland under that of St. Andrew—England under that of St. George. So also cities were placed under the care of saints, and their relics were esteemed as imparting far greater security against assault than cannon, walls, or bulwarks. Constantine, you know, defended the town of Nisibis with the dead body of St. James; and when the Emperor Leo desired to secure the relics of Simon the Stylite from Antioch, for the purposes of defence, the prudent citizens replied, "Our city has no walls, and we have brought here the holy body of Simon, that it might serve us in the stead of walls and bulwarks." And so individuals are placed under a guardian saint, or they select one for themselves. I remember, when a boy, I had one myself; but his name I am utterly unable to recall. I have no doubt but that you will say he took bad care of me.

There is, I learn, an authentic list of the relics, deemed true, possessed and published by your church. I have never seen it. It must be a very curious book. In the absence of your catalogue, I select a few of the relics greatly venerated by papists, from books of authority that lie before me. They are almost as amusing as your miracles. I will omit those too offensive to be named, out of respect for you, my readers, and myself.

The arms, legs, fingers, toes of the saints are greatly multiplied. There are eight arms of St. Matthew, three of St. John, and almost any number of St. Thomas a-Becket. There are in the Church of Lateran, the ark made by Moses in the wilderness, the rod of Moses, and the table on which the last supper was instituted by the Saviour. The table is entirely at Rome; but there are many pieces of it in other places. On the altar of the Lateran are the heads of Peter and Paul entire, but there are pieces of them in Bilboa, greatly honored by the monks. St. Peter's Church is blessed with the cross of the penitent thief; with the lantern of Judas; with the dice used by the soldiers in casting lots for the Saviour's garments; with the tail of Balaam's ass; and with the axe, saw, and hammer of St. Joseph. Different churches are enriched with pieces of the wood of the cross; and were the pieces all brough. together, they would make a hundred crosses. In one church is some of the manna in the wilderness; in another some blossoms from Aaron's rod; in another an arm of St. Simon; in another the picture of the Virgin, painted by Luke—in another one of her combs; in another the combs of the apostles, but little used; in another a part of the body of St. Lazarus, that smells; in another a part of the Gospel of Mark, in his own handwriting; in another a finger of St. Ann, the Virgin's sister; in another St. Patrick's stick, with which he drove venomous reptiles from Ireland; in another some of St. Joseph's breath, caught by an angel in a vial; in another a piece of the rope with which Judas hung himself; in another some of the Virgin's hair—in another some of her milk. And the monks once showed among their relics the spear and shield with which Michael encountered the dragon of Revelation; and some relic-monger had a feather from the wing of the Holy Spirit, when taking the form of a dove he abode upon Christ at his baptism! On the miracles wrought by the relics of the saints I have already sufficiently dwelt. They are various, and very numerous.

I will not, I cannot, here dwell upon the awful abuses of your doctrine of relics; on the robbery of all kinds of graves in Palestine, and the hawking of pilfered bones all over Europe; on the selling of old wood, sufficient to warm a small town through the winter, as pieces of the cross; on the selling of hands and feet of particular saints, until the proof is positive that some of the favored ones had as many hands as Briareus, and as many feet as the crawling worm we call the centipede. I turn from the abuse to the doctrine.

Now, Sir, where is the origin of your doctrine of relics? Can you find a trace of it in the New Testament? Will you, for a moment, compare the sham miracles wrought at the tombs of some of your saints with that wrought by the bones of a prophet of Israel? Will you dare to say that the curing of a sore throat, by a dead man's hand, is to be placed on the same ground with the miraculous cures of the apostles? I venerate the names, I would even decorate the tombs of the good; but what virtue is there in a bone from the body of Paul or Peter? or in a slip of wood from the cross? or in a strand from the rope with which Judas hung himself? or in some hairs from the tail of the beast which Balaam whipped.

If relics ever performed miracles, why do they

not perform some now? Is the virtue of all your old bones exhausted? Where is the holy coat of Treves? Where now are the pilgrims to the bones of Becket? Where is your shop in New-York for the sale of holy teeth, and holy fingers, and holy bones, taken from the graves of the saints? Sir, the whole matter is one of the vilest impositions ever practised upon the credulity of man. I do not charge you with believing a word of it. I could almost as soon believe in the virtue of the paring of the toe-nails of some of your saints, as admit that a man of your high sense can believe in these things.

But I must hasten to a brief consideration of your doctrine of *indulgence*. And how shall I characterize it?

Your church teaches that sins of a certain character deserve temporal and eternal punishment. Penance secures the remission of the latter; indulgence releases from the former. So that indulgences secure a release from the debt of temporal punishment.

No person but a lineal descendant of St. Peter can grant an indulgence. And that all such have the power of granting them, is clearly proved, by the fact that the Saviour gave the keys to Peter, and told him that whatsoever he bound or loosed on earth should be bound or loosed in heaven.

Indulgences can be only granted to those who have, by penance, secured the remission of eternal punishment; and they can be granted even to such only for a good cause or motive. Unless the cause or motive is *a good one*, heaven does not loose what the bishop looses. The causes or motives deemed good are, "the doing of great works for the glory of God and the public benefit of the church, such as the propagation of the catholic faith, building churches, alms, &c." And the way in which the bishop secures the remission of the temporal punishment of the indulged one,—he draws upon the satisfaction of Christ and his saints, called "the treasure of the church," and offers the draft to God, as an equivalent for the punishment due to the individual! I do think that some heated controversialists have distorted this doctrine of your church; but you will not say that this is a distortion of it. It is taken, almost literally, from Challoner and Milner.

The illustration of Milner, of the working of the thing, is a curiosity in its way. It is drawn from 2 Sam., 12th chapter. David, by the murder of Uriah, and by adultery with his wife, incurred both eternal and temporal punishment. He confessed to Nathan and did penance, and eternal punishment was remitted. The temporal yet remained, and he suffered it all. And why? There was no priest or bishop to grant him indulgence!

Such, Sir, is your doctrine of indulgence. Permit me to give you my thoughts in reference to it.

There is not a shadow of authority for it in the Scriptures. The church has authority to receive hose she deems worthy of membership, and to cast out offenders. And when offenders, cast out from her bosom, have given due evidence of repentance, she has the power of again receiving them; she is bound to do so. Upon this simple scriptural position your church has erected the sacrament of penance, and the doctrine of indulgence!

Nor have you a shadow of authority for prescribing a meritorious satisfaction to God, in lieu of the penalty annexed to his law, and pronounced against sin. I have already examined and exploded your claims as to the power of the keys, and as to binding and loosing. So unreasonable, I may say, so foolish are they, that their assertion only exposes you to ridicule. Let us suppose that David were now king of the State of New-York, with the sins of the matter of Uriah fresh upon him: could you go to him and say, "May it please your majesty, I John Hughes, by the power of binding and loosing transferred to me by Peter, will grant you indulgence from the temporal punishment due to your sins; and that child born to you by the wife of Uriah shall live, by virtue of my indulgence, if you only build for me a splendid cruciform church, and endow it with regal magnificence?" Should you do this, would not your conduct be branded, not only as revoltingly arrogant, but as blasphemous? And is not this the way that many of your churches were built and endowed?

But you now lower your tone, and say, that indulgences only remit the temporal punishment inflicted by the church. But how does this mend the matter? By your power of binding or loosing, you can send a man to hell or to heaven; you can inflict any punishment you see fit; and you can demand of the penitent, for indulgence, any "good works" you see fit. Here, sir, is the key which unlocks a chamber in your church filled with rottenness and putrefaction, more foul and filthy than the world has ever seen. Need I revert to the traffic in indulgences so zealously promoted by your popes in past days? Need I point you to their wholesale manufacture by your popes—to their selling them by wholesale to tribes of vagabond monks, who hawked them all over Europe at prices to suit purchasers? The pope drove as good a bargain as he could with the monks, and the monks with the people. For the indulgence which a poor peasant could purchase for a few pennies, a prince must pay pounds. The common sense of the world was insulted; the yoke of Rome became too heavy for the nations longer to bear; a poor monk discovered a copy of the Bible, and its truths filled his mind and his soul; strong in the Lord, he went out from his dark cell with the lamp of life in his hand; the Reformation follows. And for the exposure of her frauds and wickedness, your church has sent that poor monk to a place where the efficacy of seven sacraments—of all masses—of all indulgences—can never reach him.

But you will say all this was the abuse of the thing. My dear Sir, your doctrines of relics and indulgences have no use—they are all abuse. Guard them as you may in your Catechisms and books, practically they are all abuse. Millions have prayed at the tombs of your saints, who never offered an intelligent prayer to God through his Son. Millions have worshipped your relics, who never worshipped God in spirit and in truth. And millions have sought deliverance from sin by your penances, and extreme unctions, and indulgences, who never sought it through the blood of Jesus Christ. And at this hour many of your churches in Rome are nothing but spiritual shops for the sale of indulgences.

The frauds which your church has practised on the world, by her relics and indulgences are enormous. If practised by the merchants of New-York, in their commercial transactions, they would send every man of them to State Prison.

By your doctrine of relics you lead the people into idolatry on the one hand—by your doctrine of indulgence you give them a license to commit sin on the other. At least this is their practical effect. It is said of the holy Sturme, the disciple of St. Winfrid, that in passing a horde of unconverted Germans, as they were bathing in a stream, he was so overpowered by the intolerable stench of sin that arose from them, he nearly fainted away. Similar is the effect of the odor of your relics and indulgences upon me. Your church must abandon them utterly before I can return to her communion.

With great respect, yours,

KIRWAN.

LETTER VII.

Unmeaningness of Romish Doctrines and Ceremonies.—Baptism—The Mass—Penance—Extreme Unction—Holy Water—Prayers to the Saints—Withholding the Scriptures.

Rev. and dear Sir :—I ask your attention in the present letter, to the consideration of another objection, which, mountain-like, opposes my return to your church, drawn from *the utter unmeaningness of your peculiar doctrines and ceremonies.* If I coin a new word to express my meaning, surely you will forgive me, a bishop in a church which has coined doctrines, and sacraments, and ceremonies, without meaning, and without end.

When I look into the New Testament, every thing there is plain and simple. True, there are some doctrines there taught, which are above my entire comprehension; but yet they are *plainly* taught. Having settled the divine authority of the Scriptures, I never question what they plainly teach. Its most mysterious truths are not opposed to my reason; they are only above it. When I look at the worship, and ceremonies there enjoined, they all seem to me perfectly simple and expressive. And so are the worship and ceremonies of almost all the Protestant churches with which I am acquainted. So far as they deviate from simplicity and expressiveness, do they deviate from the apostolical model.

But when I turn to your church—the church of my fathers,—every thing peculiar to it wears a contrary aspect, and to my mind seems utterly unmeaning, and frequently absurd. Permit me to illustrate what I mean. And even should I occupy this letter with my illustrations, my only excuse to you and my readers is, the importance of the subject.

I begin with your sacrament of Baptism. This we all admit to be a sacrament; but I have now to do with the power and significancy which you give it, and the ceremonies you connect with it.

The effects of baptism when duly administered, as stated by Challoner, are these:—It washes away original sin—it remits all actual sin—it infuses the habit of divine grace into the soul—it gives a right and title to heaven—it makes us children and members of the church. Now, Sir, I have no sense by which I can perceive how the application of water by a priest, or a minister, or a laic, or a midwife, can accomplish all this, whilst testimony to the contrary addresses itself to all my senses. Christ died for the sins of all that believe in him—it is faith in Christ that secures the washing away of original and actual sin—and faith is the exercise of a heart renewed by the Holy Ghost. Being justified by faith, we have peace with God and a title to heaven. All this I can understand; but how your dipping three times in water can do all this, I see not. What the Bible attributes to the Holy Spirit, and to the exercise of true faith, you claim for the sacrament of baptism

If your doctrine of baptismal regeneration is true, what a singular commentary we have of it in the lives of your people! What singular manifestations of the habits of divine grace which your baptism infuses into the soul, you see daily among your people! I only wonder that the facts in the case have not long since exploded your doctrine, and led you back to the simplicity of the sacrament as taught in the Bible! The apostles administered baptism to those who confessed faith in Jesus Christ; and through this sacrament we obtain a place and a name in the visible church. This all men can understand; but how you, or any mortal man, by the application of water in any or all ways, can wash away the original and actual sins of the sinner,—infuse into his soul the habits of grace, and give him a title to heaven, I cannot comprehend. If your baptism could only do this, it would wonderfully mend the habits of many of your people, and save some of the criminal courts of New-York a world of trouble!

And the power you claim for it is no more unmeaning than the ceremonies you connect with it. This sacrament, ordinarily, must be administered in churches with fonts, whose water must be blessed "on the vigils of Easter and Whitsunday." There must be godfathers and godmothers. The priest blows in the face of the subject of baptism thrice, to drive Satan out of him! Then blessed salt is pu in his mouth! Then ex orcism is performed to drive the devil out of him! This is all done in the porch of the church. Then he is introduced into the church, where prayers are said. Then the priest puts his spittle on his ears and nose. Then he is anointed with holy oil, "blessed on Maunday-Thursday." And then he is baptized. Then he is anointed on the top of the head with holy chrism. Then a white linen cloth is placed on his head. Then a lighted candle is put in his hand! Then the ceremony is ended, and the person is dismissed, his sins all washed away—the habits of grace infused into his soul, and his title to heaven in his pocket!

Now, sir, excite my wits as I may, I cannot understand all this. It is addressed to my ignorance.

The whole ceremony of your *Mass* is yet more unmeaning to me. Often as I have witnessed it, I never gleaned one intelligent idea from it—nor does one out of one million of your people. I have just read through the laboured explanation of it by Bishop England; and it is truly painful to see so noble a mind expending its powers in the vain attempt to give meaning to every thread of such a gossamer web;—to give sense and significance to what is so utterly nonsensical.

"In the Mass," says Dr. England, "Christ is the victim; he is produced by the consecration, which, by the power of God, and the institution of the Redeemer, and the act of the priest, place the body and blood of Christ, under the appearance of bread and wine, upon the altar; then the priest makes an oblation of this Victim to the Eternal Father on behalf of the people, and the victim undergoes a destructive change, showing forth the death of the Redeemer, and making commemoration thereof, by the exhibition of the apparent separation of the body from the blood; the former being under the appearance of bread, and the latter under the appearance of wine, and by the consumption of both by the priest." This is, on the whole, the clearest account of the mass that I have ever seen from the pen of a priest; and yet what mind can understand it? Sir, do you understand it? Christ produced from some bread and wine by a priest—this produced Christ is laid upon the altar by the priest—an oblation of this produced Christ is made to the Eternal Father by the priest—the produced Christ undergoes a destructive change in the act of oblation—this oblation of the produced Christ is offered for the people—and then this produced, offered Christ, and after he has undergone a destructive change, is eaten by the priest! Sir, all this is as umeaning to me as the leaves which the fabled sybil scattered on the winds. And this unmeaning Mass, a greater mass of absurdity than ever heathen ingenuity or depravity invented, is the chief source of edification to the nine-tenths of the papal world! If it were merely unmeaning, without being blasphemous and wicked, I could extend to it some toleration.

And the absurdity of the whole thing is increased

to intensity by the fact that the pantomime is performed in Latin! Pray, Sir, how many of your worshippers at St. Patrick's understand English, not to say Latin? Why use a language, now no longer spoken by any nation or people, which is now simply a medium of intercourse among scholars? The answer given to this question by Challoner, is one of the most cool insults that I have ever known offered to the common sense of the world. Here it is:—1. Because it is her ancient language . . . and the church, which hates novelty, desires to celebrate her liturgy in the same language;—2. For a greater uniformity in public worship; that a papist, wherever he wanders, may witness the ceremonies of the mass in the same language;—3. To avoid the changes to which all vulgar languages are exposed. He also tells us that it is unnecessary to understand what we are saying, if our hearts are only sincere! Sir, I see not how men who offer, or receive such statements as reasons, can have the faculty of understanding a reason. Because the ritual of the Mass was first formed in Latin; because Mass was first said in Latin at Rome, the hatred of your church to novelty forbids her to change the language of her ritual, when there is not a congregation on earth that can understand it! And it is not necessary to understand the language in which we address ourselves to God, if we only intend to worship him! And such is the excuse you make for the man who may be worshipping a false relic for a true one. If he only means to honour the true relic, it makes no difference! If he mistakes the thigh of Barabbas for that of Barnabas; or the finger of Pilate for that of Peter; or the hair of Jezebel for that of Mary; or the head of Balaam's ass for that of Paul, it is all the same, if he only means to worship the true relic! And I suppose the difference, Sir, is very little.

These things may be very clear to you and to your priests, and people; but to me they are utterly without meaning, save a meaning that insults my common sense.

And such is the fact as to your doctrine of Penance, and Extreme Unction, which I have already examined. I am a sinner. To obtain forgiveness, you tell me that I must confess to you—that I must perform the penances you enjoin—that I must secure absolution from you—and that until all this is done, I cannot procure forgiveness. Now I cannot understand how this process secures for me what I desire. I readily understand how, if I confess my sins to God, and forsake them, and rest with true faith on his Son, I can obtain forgiveness. But your doctrine of penance, and its reputed efficacy, are as difficult for me to understand as they are contrary to the Bible.

And so as to your Extreme Unction. I am in a dying state. The sands in my glass are almost run. You come to my dying bed with your little cup of olive oil, blessed on Maunday-Thursday. Dipping your thumb in the box, you cross and anoint my eyes, my nose, my tongue, my ears, my hands, my feet, and when the crossing and anointing is over, I am prepared for "the port of eternal happiness." Now, Sir, after every effort, I cannot understand how olive oil produces those effects, if rubbed on with both your thumbs, and with all your fingers. I can readily see how the blood of Christ applied to my soul in the dying hour by the Holy Spirit, fits it for its departure; but how olive oil, or any other oil, rubbed on by your thumb, or poured upon me in a deluge, can effect this, is a mystery utterly beyond my power of solving.

And to whichsoever of your peculiar doctrines or ceremonies I turn, I find the same unmeaningness in them all.

I go into your church, St. Patrick's. I go with the multitude to the stone basin containing the holy water, and dipping my fingers into it, I cross myself with the water. This water is made holy by being exorcised by the priest, mixed with salt, and then prayed over. And I cross myself with it that it may defend me from the power of the devil! Now, Sir, all this I cannot understand. The devil is cast out of the water—then the water is salted—then it is consecrated—and then I am required to sprinkle myself with it in order to keep off the devil. I can readily see how salt will keep the water from becoming putrid, but how you get Satan out of the water, and how the water can keep Satan away from me, is beyond my comprehension. And where do you get this rite of holy water? I remember, when a boy, seeing the priest on Sunday passing through a densely crowded chapel, with two boys carrying a tub of holy water before him, and he sprinkling it upon the people with something which I then thought was a cow's tail. And if that water drove the devil out of some of them that I well remember, I would like to know how they acted when he was in them. If holy water would only produce the effects which you attribute to it, I would wish you to give many of our countrymen a pretty thorough sprinkling.

I find the same difficulty in your doctrine which teaches me to pray to the Saints. How Paul or Peter can hear me in New-York, and another in Cork, praying to them at the same time, passes my comprehension. I am sure poor Mary must have her hands full if she attends to all who supplicate her favor. I have no doubt that, in the papal world, ten pray to her, where one prays to God.

Nor can I comprehend why, or for what purpose, you withhold from me the free use of the Scriptures. They are a revelation from God to man—not to priests only, but to the race. They are the chart of the way to life, and all men are commanded to search them. Why not permit, command all men to search them? The shipping merchant furnishes his captains with charts of all the seas over which they are to sail, and enjoins a constant use of them; and you take from me the chart which God has given me to direct me across the ocean of life, and to a safe anchorage beneath the shelter of the Rock of Ages. Why is this?

My dear Sir, God has given me a mind to understand his will; and in revealing his will to me he has consulted the intelligence with which he has endowed me. He asks of me an intelligent service and worship. He requires all men to worship him in spirit and in truth.—Your church requires me to deny the testimony of my senses—to go contrary to the decisions of my reason—to believe, not only without, but against, evidence,—to believe in doctrines as true, which common reason pronounces absurd, and to submit to ceremonies which would seem solemn were they not so ludicrous and farcical. I believe it is Thomas Aquinas, who proves the duty of inferiors to submit to superiors in the church, from the very pertinent passage in Job, "the oxen were ploughing and the asses feeding beside them." And whilst I have no objection to your bishops and priests considering themselves oxen, I prefer, on the whole, a religion, to believe and practice which does not require me to be turned into a donkey.

With great respect, yours,

KIRWAN.

LETTER VIII.

The destiny of the Papacy—Its growth—Its history not yet written – The Reformation—Reasons for the extinction of popery—1. Incapable of reformation—2. Its reformation impossible—3. Opposed by the intelligence of the world—4. By its piety.—5. The causes which gave it origin passing away—6. Its extinction ordained—7. How it is to be done.

My Dear Sir :—In my last letter I brought to a close the chief objections which prevent my return to your church. As they bear, at least, upon my own mind, you and all men will say that they are insurmountable. If I have misstated any of your doctrines—if I have magnified any of their absurdities—I have done it ignorantly. And if I have uttered a sentence that could have been avoided in the discussion, and that can be interpreted as personally offensive or disrespectful to yourself, I regret it. I feel proud of you as a countryman ; I sincerely respect your character ; and the only feeling in my soul in reference to you is, one of deep, I might almost say, agonizing regret, that you should lend your talents, character, and influence to the sustaining of such a system of delusion as is popery, which I deem equally at war with the Bible and with the common sense and best interests of men. However much or little value you place on this avowal, it is made in sincerity. In the present letter, which will close those addressed to you personally, I will ask your attention to *some considerations bearing on the ultimate destiny of your church.*

The growth of your church has been like that of the mustard seed—small in its beginning, but gradually unfolding, until its branches overshadowed the world. It took centuries, and generations of men endowed with all the deceivableness of an unrighteous policy, to perfect its despotic unity. Corruption was introduced so gradually as to create no general alarm. And the truth of God was so mixed up with the traditions of men, as to take away the power of the truth, and as to rivet upon the world the traditions of men as the commandments of God; and the whole system was so adapted to the tendencies of our fallen nature, as to gain easy access for it into barbarous and semi-civilized states. From being an ally of the state, it rose to the government of the state. It put out, first, the lights of civil, and then of religious liberty. By it kings reigned, and princes decreed judgment. And by the silent and gradual deposit of corruption and power, your church rose, a vast form and complicated, of superstition, error, and tyranny, shutting out the light of heaven from the mind, and the hope of heaven from the soul, and filling the world with the gloom and terror of its despotism. O, Sir, the history of your church, from the seventh to the seventeenth century, is yet unwritten. Much has been revealed, but the one-half has not been told us. Nor will man ever know, until the day of final revealing, a tithe of the miseries and woes which it has inflicted on our race. When the pall of darkness which now conceals them will be drawn aside, and when in all their crimson hues they will be exposed to the gaze of a collected universe—when the martyrs from the "Alpine Mountains cold"—and from the vales of Piedmont—and from the dungeons of the Inquisitions—when the Huguenots of France, and slaughtered Protestants of the isles and the continents shall all rise up and testify against her, where can popes, prelates, and priests then find a hiding place? The rocks and mountains, disregarding their cries, will not fall upon them, nor hide them from the face of an angry God.

The world bore the burden of the despotism of your church until it could be borne no longer. The Reformation ensued; and because God was in it, the combined efforts of popes, emperors, kings, and prelates failed to arrest it. All the elements of superstition, and depravity, and selfishness, and cupidity, and of civil and ecclesiastical power, were moved to their deep foundations, and were combined with unsurpassed skill to suppress it, but in vain. The nations broke the heavy yoke which your church had placed upon their necks, and indignantly cast it away. And from that day until this, the conflict has continued between Protestantism and Popery—between the law of Christian liberty and of Papal thraldom—between the principles of an open Bible, and the free access of the soul to God through a Mediator, and of a closed Bible, and the religion of sacraments, and ceremonies, and priestly interferences without meaning, measure, or end. It must be confessed, that in this conflict your church has retained its ground with great art and skill, and that after three hundred years of hard fighting it yet is in the field, and with a fearful array. But what is her destiny? Is she to rise again to her former power, and to tread out the liberty of the world, and to send us all to school again to muttering monks, and to open hell to all who decline her authority, and to admit to heaven only those whose great faith or great ignorance receives all that she teaches? Sir, I have no fear of this. I am most firmly persuaded that your church is destined to total extinction. And permit me, in the briefest manner, to state to you a few of the reasons which sustain me in this belief.

1. Your church is incapable of reformation. What may be reformed may be preserved: but the diseased body that allows no purgatives to remove its fever, and no stimulants to quicken its decaying organs, must die. And your church is just such a body. Because infallible, it has never fallen into error in doctrine or in practice. So that what it once believes and commands is always true, and is always binding. Infallibility forbids reformation. Here, then, is the position which it holds before the world—an infallible church—its sense and nonsense equally true and important—and because infallible, incapable of reformation! And, in my opinion, it is well it is so. This very position will hasten its overthrow.

How soon were the waters of the sea made the winding-sheet of the Pharaoh that, amid the wonders which were wrought around him, refused to lessen the burdens of Jacob and to let Israel go! Old Baxter was in the habit of saying, "What will not bend must be broken."

2. Even if the doctrine of your church permitted reformation, any reformation is impossible, save that which ends in its extinction. I refer, of course, to a reformation of your *system*, and not to that of individuals. How can your doctrine as to the pope's supremacy be reformed, save by its utter abandonment? How reform your transubstantiation—your purgatory—your penance—your extreme unction—your praying to dead men and women—your relic worship? No reformation of these things is possible. How can they be re-formed? If they cannot be, they must be abandoned; and if abandoned, where is your church? Gone, like the fabric of a vision, which leaves not a wreck behind. And again, I say, it is well that it is so; these things will hasten its overthrow.

3. The intelligence of the world is in opposition to your church. The mind of man, wherever enlightened, and permitted to act freely, is opposed to it. The most enlightened, the most commercial nations, are anti-papal. The literature of the world is against it. The genius of history is revealing its past wickedness; the genius of romance is holding it up to ridicule by its magic creations; the genius

of poetry is rehearsing its cruelties in undying song. Nor do I now remember a living apologist for popery out of the ranks of your priesthood, worth naming, save Chateaubriand, whose eloquent work, "Génie du Christianisme," is much more of a romance than a serious apology for your system. And all this whilst the historian—the poet—the novelist—the essayist—the penny-a-liner—the grave quarterly—the lighter monthly—the laughing weekly, are out in opposition to it.

4. The prayers and the piety of the world are against it. I assert this as a rule which has its exceptions—exceptions within the pale of your own church, where, I believe, in spite of your system, there are some of whom the world is not worthy. But from tens of thousands of hearts, in every land upon which the sun shines, the prayer is daily ascending to heaven that popish superstition may come to a perpetual end. And God is a prayer-hearing God.

5. The causes which gave rise to your church are rapidly passing away. Popery, you know, for the most part, rose in times of great ignorance. As the art of printing was unknown, the Bible was but little circulated. It required almost a lifetime to transcribe it, and a large fortune to purchase it. Hence your priests could teach almost any thing for divine truth, because the people had no Bible by which to test their teaching. And having enormously multiplied, for doctrines, the commandments of

men, it became your settled policy, as far as possible, to suppress the free use of the Bible. This is all over with you; and the Bible will be soon in every living language and among all people. And the ignorance of those ages in which the foundations of your church were laid is passing away. The schoolmaster is going into all the earth; and, with an instructed mind and an open Bible, the priest will not be long endured as a substitute for the preacher, nor the saying of mass for the proclamation of the glorious gospel of salvation. Despotic governments, too, which lent the power of the state to the priest, to assist him in riveting the chains of bondage on the people, are becoming more free. In many nations they have passed, in many more they are passing, away. The old feudal system and popery formed the upper and the nether millstone, in the mill in which the people were ground down to the state requisite to suit your purposes. One of these stones, the feudal system, is broken. It will require all your wits to go on grinding with the other.

In addition to all this, intercourse among the nations is rapidly increasing. By the power of steam the most distant people are made neighbors; and by the application of magnetism the thoughts of men are made to travel round the earth, with a velocity far surpassing that of the sun. That stagnation of mind, and of the mass, which is the true element of popery, as of all superstition, is broken up; and at the prospect of a steam engine whistling through

Italy on a railway, the papal world is alarmed. And thus the causes which gave rise to your church, and whose continuance for so many ages enabled it to maintain its fearful pre-eminence, are rapidly passing away. It would seem as if, for the last four hundred years, *every thing* was operating against her. The sacking of Constantinople—the discovery of the art of printing, and of the mariner's compass, and of this new world—the Reformation by Luther—the firmness and the weakness of princes—the periods of war and peace—the passing away of old and the rise of new dynasties—the virtues and the vices of popes, prelates, and priests—their learning and their ignorance—bloody and bloodless revolutions—the pragmatic sanction of Charles VII.—the revocation of the Edict of Nantz, by Louis XIV.—the irruptions of infidelity, and the revivals of true religion, all, all have been directed by the hand of God, so as to weaken the foundations, and as to hasten the desired period of her final fall.

6. And more than all this, it is my strong conviction that God has ordained the total extinction of your church. I will not detain you, Sir, nor my readers, with any dissertations upon the prophecies bearing on this point—this would be aside from my object. John, when wrapt in vision in Patmos, informs us that Babylon "shall be utterly burned with fire," and calls upon God's people to "come out of her," that they might not be partakers of her sins, nor receive of her plagues. And Paul tells us that the

Lord shal. consume "that wicked" with the spirit of his mouth, and des.roy him with the brightness of his rising. And by "Babylon," and "that wicked," I believe Paul and John mean the papal church. It has already lost its civil power. Once she could dethrone kings, and absolve subjects from their allegiance: now, in a civil point of view, there is no weaker power upon earth. Metternich can send his Austrian troops into the States of the Church without fearing the least injury from the successor of Gregory the Great! How is the mighty fallen! Ronge in Germany, excited to opposition by the impositions of the holy coat of Treves, has led out one hundred thousand from the yoke of your church; and all that his Holiness can do is, to bear it. Even in the city of New-York, the resolute Germans are flocking out from the care of Holy Mother; and all that you can do is, to flourish your crook, your keys, and your crosier around the altar of St. Patrick's, without the least power to stop one of the wandering sheep. The temporal power of your church is gone; the spiritual is fast going after it. And the time will soon be here, when the pen of the historian will write, THE CHURCH OF ROME WAS, BUT IS NOT.

How this is to be done, is a question of some importance, and upon which I have my own opinions. A careful looking at past providences may cast some light upon the future, and inspire hope or fear, according to the relation we sustain to God and his church You know, Sir, the way in which God treated Pharaoh, and the Canaanites, and how he blotted out the nations that opposed the progress of his people. You know the way and manner in which he broke up the Jewish church and state, for their opposition to Christ and his church! You know how the Reformation progressed, from small beginnings, until it opened a new epoch in the world's history—from what was considered a little ecclesiastical gladiatorship, until kingdoms were shaken—until thrones, cemented by ages, were convulsed and tottered to their base—until hostile armies met in deadly combat, and fattened the earth with the blood of the Papist and the Protestant. God has the control of all agencies to accomplish his will. Much will be done for the extinction of your church by education—much by the general influence of learning—much, very much by the circulation of the Bible—much more by the simple and fervent preaching of the gospel to the masses, as did Luther—and much by the direct agency of Him, in whose sight the nations are as a drop in the bucket, and who will overturn and overturn, until He shall come whose right it is to reign.

These, Rev. Sir, are in brief my reasons for bebelieving that your church is destined to utter extinction. No reasons can be drawn for its future continuance, from its continuance until now. If your people had not been papists, they might have been pagans or infidels. The Canaanites remained a long time in the land to perplex the Jews. Paganism continued for ages in the Roman world, after its conversion to Christianity. Yet both became extinct, save as paganism has been perpetuated by your people. Nor can any argument be drawn from the occasional conversions to your communion which are now occurring. You know that in ages past some Christian ministers relapsed into idolatry; and that during the French Revolution some of your bishops, and many of your priests, went over to infidelity. You must lay no flattering unction to your soul from arguments like these. Your church is opposed to the truth of God—to the people of God—to the will of God. The shed blood of the martyrs is crying to heaven against it. Its extinction is certain; and may God hasten it, in his own time and way.

With the most sincere prayers for your temporal and eternal welfare, I remain, with great respect,

Your fellow-countryman and fellow-sinner,

KIRWAN.

LETTER IX.

To all, and especially to American, Roman Catholics:

My dear Friends,—Having addressed a series of letters to one of your most celebrated and excellent bishops in this country, the Right Reverend John Hughes, of New York, candidly stating the reasons which induced me to abandon the Roman Catholic Church, and which prevent my return to it, I desire, before I lay aside my pen, perhaps never to be resumed on this subject, to address myself to you. And I turn from the bishop to you, for various reasons, some of which I desire in the briefest manner to state.

1. Whilst entirely honest, I believe you to be a people deluded by your priests. They have taken from you the Bible—they forbid you to reason on the subject of religion—they have filled your minds with prejudices against all who resist or question their authority—they have imposed upon you for doctrines the commandments of men—and they have impressed upon you the belief that with them is the power to admit or to exclude you from heaven. In stating these things I say what I do know, and what you know. With me it is no theory, for I have felt it all.

2. I believe you to be a people impoverished and

degraded by your priests. The reasons for my opinion on this subject are stated in the preceding letters. Ignorance being the parent of papal devotion, the priests have shut out from you the ligh of knowledge. Ignorance begets vice, and vice is the parent of poverty. Or if ignorance begets not vice, it is the rank soil in which superstition attains its most magnificent growth. And which most degrades a people, vice or superstition, it is not worth the while to inquire. I verily believe it impossible to be a true papist without sinking the man.

3. I believe that the papal world need look for no redress of grievances, for no true reformation, from its prelates or priests. The history of the world, and the history of the church, and the principles of human nature, forbid us to entertain the idea. How few and far between, the instances in which despotic kings, or rulers, of their own accord, retrenched their expenditures to relieve the burdens of their subjects, or yielded their usurped rights to increase the liberty of their people. And what of civil liberty the nations possess, has cost the people ages of contest with tyrants, and rivers of blood.

And when have high ecclesiastics ever led the way in salutary reformation? Not at the advent of Jesus Christ. It was the High Priest that sat in Moses' seat, and his subordinates that nailed to the cross the Lord of glory. It was the commission of the high priest to persecute the dissenters at Damascus from the order established at Jerusalem, that

Saul of Tarsus carried in his pocket, when he was arrested by heaven. The Reformers of the sixteenth century, whom your priests delight to dishonor, but yet who have given civil and religious liberty to the world, were hunted, as by bloodhounds, by the high ecclesiastics of their day. Every religious reform of permanent utility, and in every land upon which the sun shines, has been in consequence of the united action of the people. There occurs not to me now an instance to the contrary.

It is not in human nature to surrender power once possessed—nor to give up a gainful traffic—nor, for the sake of benefiting or enriching the mass, to yield up privileges. Grace leads to many sacrifices to do good to men; but nature holds on to the privileges of order, station, cast, however they may bear upon the people; and if ever the people are freed from them, it must be by their own acts. Roman Catholics! you have nothing to expect from your priests, but the perpetuation of their bad dominion over your mind and conscience; and their vigilant and united efforts to crush every man, and every influence, that would weaken it. The principles of your church forbid its reformation—a true reformation would be the end of it—there is no alternative for you but to abandon it.

These are the reasons, Roman Catholics, why I turn to you, and why I would implore you, by all that is to be desired in a mind free to think,—in a soul free to love and to act,—free in its access to

God without priestly taxes and interferences;—by all that is to be desired in the social and religious elevation of your children, and in the moral regeneration of your race, to rise, and to fling from around you the chains forged in the dark ages, and with which priests would bind you to their footstools in this age of light.

You must remember that your position in these United States is very different from what is that of those yet living in the papal countries of Europe. Here you are free to think, and act for yourselves. In Ireland you might be afraid of the priest's whip, or of his cursing you from the altar. I have seen myself a priest whip a man in the street; and I have heard the same priest curse the same man from the altar. But, here, his whip has no terror, and his curses are harmless.

And, then, as to those of you from Ireland, you are in a very different position, as to the Protestant community, from what you were at home. Protestants here are your friends. You are not taxed to support a religion you hate. Your cow or your pig are not driven from your door to pay your tithes. There is nothing here to chafe your mind, or to irritate your feelings, or to give cause to your priests for fiery appeals to your passions. Whatever may be the feelings of wicked men towards you, there is not a pious Protestant in the land that would not do you good, and that would not interpose to protect you from wrong. So that the hostile feelings towards Protestants which had an excuse in Ireland, have no excuse here. If you wish to think for yourselves there are thousands to defend you ;—and if, on examination, you think as I do about popery, and quit the church, you have nothing to fear from priestly anathemas hurled at you, or after you, from the altar; nor from an ignorant rabble that would persecute you as an apostate.

There is one point, my friends, to which I would direct your special attention. From your cradle you have been taught to regard your priests as possessing peculiar spiritual powers which you resist at your peril. And in every way and form they seek to impress you with the belief that they possess such powers, and that their communication with heaven is beyond that of ordinary mortals. Now this is an old device, and one that is practiced very widely for the purpose of awing the common and vulgar mind. Thus did the ancient priests of Egypt, who taught the people to worship the sun, the cow, the cat, and the snake. Thus do the priests of Brahma at the present day. Some of them, by their pretended intercourse with heaven, have become so holy that the people consider the water in which they wash their feet holy, and seek to be sprinkled with it with intense earnestness. The Calmucs believe in a priesthood, all of which is united in Lama, who is absorbed in deity. The old Romans had their priests, and their oracles, that were regarded as knowing and declaring the mind of the gods. Their power over the people was immense. And when pagan Rome became papal it was a point greatly desired to retain the power of the pagan priest over the people in the hands of the papal. It was attained; and it has been retained. And the power claimed by your priests for the better subjecting you to their yoke, is the power claimed by all the priests of heathenism and Mahometanism, and for the very same purpose. It is the claim of fanatics and impostors in all climes and among all people. And whether set up on the banks of the Ganges, or of the Tiber;—on the shores of the Bosphorus, or on the banks of the Hudson, its object is to exalt the priest that he may govern the people. Your priests have no more power with God than any good man in the land,—nor as much, unless they are equally pious. If not pious and sincere, they are simply impostors, who make a living by their traffic in your souls.

Once secure a just and scriptural view of the character of a true minister of Christ, and of the great end of a gospel ministry, and the whole framework of popery vanishes. The end of the gospel ministry is, to hold up a crucified Christ as God's great remedy for the sins, and guilt, and woes of our race, and so to expound the moral state of the sinner, and the adaptedness of the work of Christ to that state, as to lead him to see that his only hope of life is in the cross, and then to beseech him, in Christ's stead, to be reconciled to God. This being the end of the ministry, a true minister is one, who, with the love of God and of the salvation of men filling his soul, goes out into all the ways which providence opens before him, preaching every where, as did Peter and Paul, "repentance towards God, and faith in our Lord Jesus Christ." He has only one object—*to lead men to the knowledge of the truth.* He carries no wafers to convert into Christs; he makes no pretensions to the power of regenerating souls by baptizing them; he calls not upon men to confess to him, but to God; he has no unmeaning masses to mutter; no relics to sell; no unmeaning rites to enjoin; no olive oil, or holy salt, or holy water, to drive away demons. He goes out, wearing no sacerdotal garments to astonish the vulgar, with an open Bible to expound it, praying that the Holy Ghost may so apply its truths to the hearts of his hearers that they may be created anew in Christ Jesus unto good works. To those who believe, he administers the rite of baptism; and as God gives him opportunity, he administers the Lord's supper to the faithful, for the purpose of commemorating the death of Christ, until he comes the second time, without sin, unto salvation. Such were the ministers of Christ before the rise of popery; and such only are the true ministers of Christ now. If so, will you bear the impositions of your priests an hour longer?

There is one other point to which I would direct your special attention, because it is one upon which you have been greatly deceived: I mean the church.

Every effort has been put forth by your priests to mystify this topic, and to deceive you in reference to it. All who truly believe in Jesus Christ, and practice the precepts of his word, are reconciled to God. They are adopted into the family of God—they are the sons and daughters of the Lord Almighty. A connexion of such with any branch of the visible church, does not interfere with their connexion with the family of God. No good man is lost, and no bad man is saved, because of their connexion with any church. As a man may be a true Papist and be a Jesuit, or a Jansenist, or a monk of La Trappe, or a shorn friar, so he may be a true Christian, and a member both of the visible and invisible church, and be a Protestant or a Papist, and a member of any of the sects into which they are both divided, which hold to the true atonement of Jesus Christ. But you will ask, Have you no preference for one branch of the church above another? I have. You ask again, What branch is it? That in which the most truth and the least error, the most simplicity and the least pompousness, exist. Of course, the very last branch I would select would be, the papal; and in the Protestant church, the very last branch I would select is, that which is most like the papal The true unity of the church is unity in the truth, and union to Christ.

Right views of the ministry of Christ, and of the church of Christ, in one hour, blow the whole fabric of popery into the air.

In this appeal to you, Roman Catholics, I am no interested party. It would not be a cent in my pocket if every man of you were to abandon the pope to-morrow; nor will it be a cent out of it if every man of you continue to believe that your priests can turn a wafer into Christ—and regenerate you by baptism—and absolve you from your sins—and get you admission to heaven, by rubbing you with olive oil, when dying. Can Bishop Hughes, or your priests say this? Why, then, you ask, this solicitude about us? On these accounts: I know you to be deceived, and I desire you to be undeceived. I know that you are led to place dependence on rites and ceremonies, for a preparation for the life to come, which give no such preparation. I know that you are robbed of your money, for services that only tend to degrade you—that you are deprived of the dearest rights of man, an open Bible, and free access to God, for yourselves, without any saintly or priestly attorneys to plead for you. I see you hampered and fettered on every hand. By telling the priest every thing you do, you put your peace and liberty into his hands. You cannot read the Bible without his license, and be a good Catholic. You cannot retain your standing, and read any book which he prohibits, or fail in any duty which he enjoins. You cannot bow your knee before God, with a Protestant, around his family altar, without the terror of a severe penance when you next go to confession. I see you freemen, in a land of freedom, and yet the veriest slaves that tread the soil, because your minds and souls are in fetters. I see you a noble people, yielding a degrading homage to men that deceive you, and sustaining, even in your poverty, with a princely liberality, institutions that degrade you. And I desire, with an irrepressible desire, to see you the subjects of the perfect law of liberty with which Christ makes his people free. These, my friends, are the reasons of my solicitude about you.

However I feel towards the system of popery, or towards the priests of the system, there is but one feeling and one desire in my heart towards you: that feeling is one of affection and interest—and that desire is, that you may be emancipated from a system of superstition and spiritual despotism, as degrading and grinding as any that God has ever permitted to exist.

With great respect, yours,

KIRWAN.

LETTER X.

Conclusion. The Indian devotee—Faith in Christ saves—The dying thief—Peter at the feast of Pentecost—The plan of Salvation—The Gospel and Papal way of Salvation contrasted—A call upon Irish Roman Catholics.

My dear Friends,—But a few years since a Christian minister in India, in the pursuit of the objects of his holy mission, met with a Hindoo devotee. A noonday sun was pouring its burning rays from a burning sky, upon the burning sands on which the meeting took place. From its heat the devotee had no protection save the piece of cloth which hung around his loins. He wore a pair of sandals pierced with iron nails, which, at every step, penetrated the muscles and nerves which are so wonderfully collected and interwoven in the soles of the feet. His sandals were filled with his blood, which marked his every footstep. He was an object frightful to behold—his body blistered by the sun, his hair clotted with filth hanging around his head, his feet swollen, bleeding and painful, almost refusing to move. The missionary asked him why he wore those sandals, and why he subjected himself to such intense suffering? He replied, that he had committed great sins which were greatly offensive to the gods, and that in order to secure the forgiveness of those sins he wore those sandals, and cheerfully submitted to all his sufferings.

Filled with compassion for the deluded man, the minister of God told him that he could show him a way in which he could secure the forgiveness of his great sins without those sandals, and without subjecting himself to such terrible sufferings. "Is there such a way, and if so, what is it?" exclaimed he devotee, with the most intense interest. "There is such a way," replied the missionary; and taking his Bible, he read to him and expounded the following passage: "For God so loved the world that he gave his only begotten Son, that whosoever believeth in him should not perish, but have everlasting life." John 3: 16. He told the poor deluded man of the sins of men—of the love of God in giving his Son to die for the sins of those who should believe on him—of the birth, and sufferings, and death, of Jesus Christ—and he especially dwelt upon this one, great, glorious, and scriptural idea, that he that believes on the Lord Jesus Christ shall be saved. The devotee heard with amazement. He believed. He rejected the false religion of his fathers, though sanctioned by a thousand ages. He renounced subjection to his priests and their traditions. He flung from him his nailed and bloody sandals, by walking in which he supposed he was saving his soul by the tortures of his body. He received Christian baptism at the hands of the man of God that taught him the more excellent way, and lived and died in the faith and hope of the Gospel.

In many respects your circumstances, Roman

Catholics, widely differ from what were those of this Hindoo devotee. You live in a land, and in an age of light. You form parts of a great community, which is penetrated in every direction by moral and religious influences. And yet in many respects your circumstances are like unto his. You are deluded by priests—you believe in their ghostly power, and your soul submits to it—you are looking to your confessions, and penances, and austerities, for salvation—you are excluded from the light of the Bible—with all simplicity and honesty you pray to saints, and to the virgin; and perform all that is laid upon you by your father confessor, and in this way, through the religion of the priest, and not through the religion of the gospel, you hope to get to heaven. But you are deceived. Your hopes are honest, but they are built upon a wrong foundation. It is not by *doing*, or *suffering*, but by *believing*, that we can attain unto the salvation of the soul. "He that believeth on the Lord Jesus Christ shall be saved, and he that believeth not shall be damned." "He that believeth on the Son hath life." Roman Catholics! my brethren and kinsmen according to the flesh, follow, then, the example of the Hindoo devotee. Give up your beads, and your Agnus Dei—your penances and ritual observances—your crosses, your confessions to men, and your holy water; and go to your Bibles and to the Saviour of the Bible. What all your rites and observances can never accomplish, simple faith in Jesus Christ accomplishes, and in the moment faith fixes itself upon a crucified Christ.

That you may see this clearly, permit me to state to you another incident. When our Lord was put to death, the wicked Jews, the more deeply to degrade him, caused him to be crucified between two thieves. One of these saw, in the convulsions of nature around him, the evidences of the divinity of Him who was hanging by his side on the cross; and whilst his companion in wickedness derided and blasphemed, he cried out from the depths of a convicted and believing soul unto Jesus, "Lord, remember me when thou comest in thy kingdom." The following is the reply of the Saviour: "To-day shalt thou be with me in paradise." Here, you see, my friends, are no penances—no prayers to saints—no holy water—no olive oil, blessed on Maunday-Thursday—no purgatory; it is simply faith in Jesus Christ, then death, and then paradise, which is only another name for heaven! What was it that opened heaven to this dying thief, and gave him admission to its happy mansions, as one of the redeemed of the Lord? It was simply faith in Jesus Christ. "He that believeth in the Lord Jesus Christ shall be saved." And the faith which opened heaven to the dying thief, will open it to you. Faith is the key which opens heaven to your souls, and not baptism, nor the eucharist, nor penance, nor extreme unction. Give up, then, your crosses and your pictures, and your dependence upon saints and sacraments, and go to Jesus

Christ for yourselves—with true hearts say, "Lord, I believe, help thou my unbelief," and life, eternal life is yours.

That you may see this clearly, permit me to state yet another incident. The Apostle Peter never said a mass in his life—he never changed a wafer into the body and blood of Christ—he never sent a poor sinner to pray to a saint or virgin—he never went into a little box, or a dark room, to hear confession. He was a simple, warm-hearted preacher, and, in his day, labored to impress upon the minds of men these two truths—that Jesus Christ was the promised Messiah, and that all that believed in him would be saved. Now, we learn from the second chapter of the Acts of the Apostles, that Peter preached to the multitudes assembled at Jerusalem to keep the feast of Pentecost, with great power. He mightily convinced them, from the Scriptures, that God had made the Jesus whom they crucified both Lord and Christ. Convicted of their deep sinfulness, by his powerful preaching, and by the Holy Spirit, multitudes crowd around him, asking, "What shall we do to be saved?" What does he say in reply? Does he tell them to go to confession—or to do penance—or to fast on Lent, or on Fridays? Does he send them to the saints, to ask their intercession? Nothing like this. What, then, does he say? "Repent, and be baptized, every one of you, in the name of Jesus Christ, for the remission of sins, and ye shall receive the gift of the Holy Ghost." They obeyed;

that is, they forsook their sins—they believed in Jesus Christ—they were baptized in his name—and on that occasion three thousand souls were added to the church.

My dear Roman Catholic friends, I once suffered just as you now do, because of my utter ignorance as to the way of forgiveness with God. I was taught all about confession, and confirmation, and penance, and saints' days, and fastings, and holy water, and saying "Hail Mary." I looked upon the priest as the door-keeper of heaven, without whose permission there was no admittance. But I knew nothing about the Bible, and was taught nothing about the work of Christ for the sinner, nor about the work of the Spirit in him. In great mercy, and in the way stated in my letters to Bishop Hughes, I became a reader of the Bible; and to my utter amazement, I found there taught, with perfect plainness, the way of salvation, which the priest had wrapped up in mystery inextricable. The wayfaring man, though a fool, may understand the way in which a soul may be saved, as taught in the Bible—it is beyond the comprehension of Gabriel, as taught by your priests. Do any of you ask, as did the heathen jailer of Philippi, when terrified by the effects of the crashing earthquake, "What shall I do to be saved?" Permit me, as a friend, who has no object in view but your temporal and eternal good, to place before you what I regard as the scriptural answer to this momentous question.

1 You must feel that you are a sinner exceedingly, in the sight of God. The Bible teaches us that we are sinners by nature and by practice. It is one thing to believe this—it is another to feel it. You must feel it. No man ever sends for a physician until he feels that he is sick. The people to whom Peter preached never asked what they should do to be saved, until "they were pricked in their heart."

2. You must feel and know that there is no way of securing the pardon of your sins, but through the redemption there is in Christ Jesus. We are expressly taught, "there is no other name under heaven given among men whereby we must be saved." Acts iv. 12. This is an idea that your mind must grasp with all its powers; and which you are in danger of letting slip, because of the way and manner in which you have been instructed, as to the efficacy of sacraments, and priestly manipulations, and ritual observances.

3. You must believe in the Lord Jesus Christ. This is the end and the sum of all the instructions of the New Testament to sinners. This is the commandment of God, that ye believe in the name of his Son. Faith brings you into a living union with Christ, for whose sake alone you are accepted and saved.

Here, then, we have the true answer to the question, "What shall I do to be saved?" You must feel that you are a sinner; and you must feel that none but Christ can save you; and in heart and soul you must cordially receive him, as made unto you of God wisdom, and righteousness, and sanctification, and redemption. A sense of sin will induce you to seek for its remedy. Christ crucified, bearing the sins of his people in his own body on the tree, is God's remedy for sin. And believing in Christ is the application of the remedy. And believing in Christ, should you die the very next hour, your soul would go, cleansed by his atoning blood, to join the general assembly and church of the first-born in heaven.

Need I stop, ere I close this letter, to place in contrast before you the gospel plan of salvation with the plan of your priests? Must not the contrast strike yourselves, as you read and ponder? You ask what you must do to be saved? The priest tells you to confess—to do penance—to pray to the saints—to keep Lent—to eat no meat on stated days—to go to mass—to torture your body. And when all this is done, when you come to die you must be anointed with olive oil, blessed on Maunday-Thursday. Nor will this do. You have then to go to purgatory, to atone for your venial sins by your own suffering, unless you are bought out by the alms and suffrages of the faithful, in paying for masses for your deliverance! What a long, and complicated, and *expensive* process! And after all, there is no telling the time when the suffrages of the faithful, or the masses of the priests, will secure your deliver ance from purgatorial fires! What a dark and fearful process!

In the face of all this, the gospel declares to you that the blood of Christ cleanses from all sin; and that whosoever believes in the Lord Jesus Christ shall be saved. It offers you a free, a full, a perfect salvation, and without any priestly interferences, and "without money and without price."

Can you hesitate a moment between the plan of the priest and the plan of the gospel? The one debases you as a man—makes you the slave of the priest, and cheats you of heaven: the other addresses you as a moral and intellectual being—sends you to the cross for yourself—gives you free access to God, and secures for you eternal life.

Irish Roman Catholics! would that I could induce you to look at this great subject in the light of the Bible. It is intimately connected with your temporal and eternal interests, and with the interests of unborn generations. When a boy, I often heard, and never but with burning indignation, of the magistrate, the tool of British power, entering the houses of the Irish suspected of disaffection, and tearing from its frame the speech of Emmet, made in reply to the question of the blood-thirsty judge that tried him, "What he had to say, why the sentence of death should not be passed against him according to law?" The British ministry felt that that speech fostered the spirit of freedom in the Irish bosom, and made every man that read it to resolve, at whatever expense, to be free; and they destroyed every copy of it that could be found, and forbad its publication. As my kindred were among the disaffected ones, I felt it to the quick, and so feel it yet. And what, think you, must be my feelings now, in the vigor of my manhood, when I see, in this free land, the descendants of those who fought at Vinegar Hill, and at Tara, permitting individuals calling themselves the priests of the religion of God, to enter their houses and take away their Bibles, and to forbid them, by the terrors of eternity, to think for themselves, on the most important of all subjects connected with their being! It is the very feeling that prompted the British spies to destroy the speech of Emmet, that now prompts your priests to destroy your Bibles. The one fostered the spirit of civil, the other of religious freedom. The British ministry wished to suppress the breathing of your fathers after civil liberty: your priests wish to suppress the breathings of you, their children, after religious freedom. And will you, the sons of noble sires, submit, in a land of freedom, to wear the galling chains of spiritual bondage? Will you submit to have these chains clanking around you to the grave—and when you die to have them bound upon your children, and for no earthly purpose but to sustain a priesthood and a hierarchy, for whose utter overthrow the civil and religious interests of the nations, and the temporal and eternal interests of our race, are calling aloud to heaven?

If so, with a slight variation, mine will be the language of the pious Jeremiah, who had the civil anu the religious welfare of his people equally at heart: O that my head were waters, and mine eyes a fountain of tears, that I might weep day and night for the blindness and folly of my people.

My letters are ended. I commit them to you, Roman Catholics, and to the blessing of Almighty God.

With great respect, yours,

KIRWAN.

BISHOP HUGHES CONFUTED.

REPLY

TO THE

RT. REV. JOHN HUGHES,

ROMAN CATHOLIC BISHOP OF NEW YORK.

BY

"KIRWAN."

THIRD SERIES.

PHILADELPHIA:

PRESBYTERIAN BOARD OF PUBLICATION,

CONTENTS.

PAGE

LETTER VII.

LETTER VIII.

LETTER IX.

LETTER X.

INTRODUCTORY NOTE.

When I ended my First Series of letters to Bishop Hughes, I hoped and thought that my part in the Romish controversy was also ended. Appeals, however, were made to me that I could not resist, for a new series, in the manner and spirit of the first. I yielded; and hence the Second Series. Pledging myself not to reply to any attacks made upon my letters, save by him to whom they were addressed, and feeling, for reasons stated, that he would not reply, I again supposed my work ended. But contrary to my expectations, the bishop twice attempted a reply, and with what spirit and success I need not inform the public. His first letters are as feeble as could be desired; his second are in the very worst spirit even of Popery, whose very best spirit has but little to recommend it. The feebleness of the first letters to Dear Reader, and the low personalities, not to say vulgarities of those addressed to Kirwan, reveal the true character of the author. They might be published by Protestants in a separate volume, which might be truly entitled, "Bishop Hughes Unmasked." Those letters are reviewed in the following pages.

My objections to the system of Popery are stated in my first and second series. They have not been answered; nor will they soon be. The bishop's reasons for adherence to the Catholic Church are reviewed and confuted in the present series. The present series pulls up the Upas tree by the roots; the former series lopped off its baleful branches; together they lay down the rootless, branchless trunk upon the earth to rot.

The arguments of these letters are not, of course, new. All that I have attempted to do is to strip the controversy of its learned heaviness; by recasting and simplifying, to bring it down to the comprehension of the common mind, and thus to prepare a Manual on the subject adapted to universal circulation. Such a manual, unless I mistake, was greatly needed by Papists and Protestants.

I commit these letters to the kind care of God. May His Spirit accompany their circulation, and render them instrumental "in lifting up from the world one of its heaviest curses."

KIRWAN.

New-York, September, 1848.

KIRWAN'S REPLY

TO THE

RIGHT REV. JOHN HUGHES

BISHOP OF NEW-YORK.

LETTER I.

Introduction—Free discussion important—Bp. Hughes commencing answering before reading Kirwan—Excuse for the charge of insincerity—Other accounts settled—Controversy on Romanism among the people—Object of these letters.

My dear Sir,—Contrary to all my expectations, and in the face of the excuses which I made for your silence, you have resolved, at length, to notice the "Letters" which I have addressed to you. The fact gives me unfeigned pleasure. It is hailed by all those interested in the development of truth, and in the exposure of error and imposture, as an omen of good. Had *you* been silent on the subject of those letters so would I have been. They were assailed by some of your papers and priests throughout the country, in a manner at once low and rude; but I made no reply. I was pledged to suffer the assaults of such assailants to pass unnoticed. You, sir, well know that by multitudes who wear the garments of religion, there are no manifestations of its grace,—that many, in religious controversy, esteem vulgar weapons the most effectual; and that many treat an opponent whose arguments they cannot refute, as did the Jews the Saviour in the palace of the High Priest, who "spit in his face, and buffeted him, and smote him with the palms of their hands." In arguments like these, your priests, especially those imported from Ireland, are well versed. Nor would it be any serious disadvantage to the cause of Protestantism if such arguments were confined to them Separating yourself from the priests over whom you flourish your crook as chief shepherd, I stated in one of my letters that should you reply, you "would reply as a scholar and a gentleman." In the same letter I also stated to you, that if you could secure time enough from your varied occupations to reply to some of my objections which forbid my return tc your church, "there was one at least that would read your reply with great pleasure." And whilst disappointed at the want of scholar-like and gentlemanly bearing of your letters, I have yet hailed them and read them with pleasure.

The history of the world, and of the progress of truth, clearly prove the exceeding importance of *free* discussion. From such discussion, conducted in a right spirit, nothing can suffer but error and imposture. This Protestantism courts, and Popery condemns where the power is in her hands. If you and

I, sir, lived in Austria, Spain, Sicily, or in the States of the Church, your reply to my letters might come, not in the Freeman's Journal, but in the way of a warrant through the civil magistrate for my imprisonment or banishment as a heretic. But here we can have free discussion to the full; and however you or your people may feel on the subject, I am persuaded that Protestants are resolved to use their privilege. And could your people think, and read, and believe, and act for themselves, without any of the terrors or trammels which your system casts around them, I feel persuaded that two generations would reduce the spiritual power of the pope your master to a yet lower point than that to which his temporal power has fallen. Hence I hail your letters as an advance toward free discussion, which has ever been the desire of Protestants, because of its tendency to the development of truth.

Permit me, in the briefest manner, and before I proceed to other statements, to allude to a few things in your introductory letter. Some of them to me, and to many of your readers, appear singular enough.

You begin by saying that you have "seen a certain work announced and much lauded in the papers, entitled "Kirwan's Letters to Bishop Hughes. I have not read these letters, though I have twice attempted to do so." And yet in the subsequent paragraphs of this letter you seem to know that Kirwan has treated you with personal respect—that he imputes to you a want of sincerity in the profession of the Catholic faith—that his letters have attracted attention "by a sprightliness of style in assailing the doctrines of the Catholic Church, which renders them a pleasing contrast to the filthy volumes that have been written on the same side, and on the same subject,"—you seem to know "the great topics which Kirwan has discussed," and that "he has published reasons for having left the Catholic Church and for refusing to return." And for these letters, which you so well understand without having ever read them, you resolve to put forth an antidote! Now, sir, you either read Kirwan's Letters, or you did not read them; if you read them why deny it? if you did not read them, how came you by such an accurate knowledge of their contents, and of their spirit? And has the world ever heard or read of a man seriously undertaking to reply to a book which he has not read? For your own sake, sir, I wish all your assumed carelessness here had more of an air of truthfulness; for there is not a man in or out of your church who reads your letter who will not say that you either read Kirwan's Letters, or that you had them read to you. And there was no need of exposing yourself to such an imputation for the unworthy purpose of expressing your contempt. I disclaim every thing personally offensive to yourself when I say that, as to truthfulness, papal priests have but little capital on which to trade, and that they should be very sparing of what they have. They are already trembling on the verge of bankruptcy.

You also complain that I do you great injustice by imputing to you a want of sincerity in your profession of belief in the Catholic faith. I felt when I made it, and now feel, that the imputation is a serious one. And yet I knew not how to withhold it; nor do I know now how to withdraw it. I can make vast allowances for ignorance; but you are not an ignorant man. So I can make great allowance for the prejudices of early training, and for the influences of a narrow and bigoted education when so conducted as to fill the mind, not with knowledge, but with error and superstition. But thus, unless I am misinformed, you have not been trained or educated. I can also make allowance for well educated and well disciplined minds that have always been excluded from contact with minds holding opposite sentiments; and that are unaccustomed to hear questioned the truth of their opinions; but this is not your case. You are no stranger to polite society—to the company of educated men. You well know that the doctrines peculiar to your church are rejected as not only unscriptural, but as unreasonable, and as absurd, by the great mass of the educated mind of our world. And how to account for your professed belief in them I knew not, and now know not. The thing came up before my mind in this wise: Does Bishop Hughes believe that a mass mumbled over, for half a dollar, will avail in getting a soul out of purgatory? does he believe that a little wafer made of flour is converted into the real body and blood of Christ, by his consecration of it? Does he believe that he can send a man to heaven by rubbing him with a little olive oil when dying? If he believes in these things he is a dunce; but he is not a dunce; therefore he does not believe them. This, sir, I frankly tell you, was the train of thought which led me to the conclusion of which you complain as an injurious imputation. There was no alternative for me but to question your sense or your sincerity; and I preferred the latter as on the whole the most pleasing to yourself. I do not know that there is a living man who would not prefer to be called a knave rather than a fool. The first simply implies a sinful misdirection of his sense, and may be the imputation of selfishness or malice; the other is a denial that he has any sense. So that the imputation, instead of "betraying the evil effects of my Presbyterian training," exhibits rather "the generous instincts of my Irish nature" in making for you the best apology that the case would admit.

I think, sir, your friends will regret the whole tone of your introductory letter, considering the courtesy which I observed towards you. It exhibits a spirit unworthy of a bishop. You could continue in silence without any one having a right to impugn your motives; but when you came forward to reply you should have exhibited less irritation.

am sorry that my letters vexed if they failed to convert you. Your conjecture and mistake, as to my name, might have been omitted. Your regrets over my Irish birth are ludicrous; your saying that you would rather I had been any body else's countryman than yours is probably among the truest things you have said. You know not why I directed my letters to you; this is owing to the fact that you commenced answering before reading them. You assert, as far as you know, that the public never asked for my reasons for leaving your church. Had I recently gone to confession to you, you might think differently. You say it is a matter of the least importance to Catholics whether I return or not. It is very likely that the sun would rise and set without either of us; it certainly did so before we were born, and may continue to do so after we are dead. It is not wise, even for a bishop, to indulge the conceit that the sun rises in his mouth and sets at his feet. But all this, sir, is aside from the great object of my letters; it is the *argumentum ad invidiam*, and is unworthy of you and of me. If my object in my letters to you—or your object in the letters of which you make mine the occasion—or the object of these letters in reply to yours, is obtained, we must omit personalities, and seek solely and only the truth. The truth only is worthy the pursuit of high-minded and Christian men.

You say, and truly, that the public mind is

awake to the relative positions of the Catholic and Protestant churches. This is emphatically so. Controversies which hitherto have been confined to universities and ecclesiastics are now down among the people. Even the Italian mind, which the evil influences of your church have almost extinguished, is questioning the truth of your dogmas and forms, and is breathing after emancipation from them. Catholic Germany is in agitation, and the aid of princes is invoked to prevent the people from becoming Protestant. The entire Catholic world is in commotion, seeking to break the fetters with which your popes and priests have bound it for ages. In this land of our adoption all minds are using the privilege of thinking freely secured to them; and where there is one Protestant that passes over to your church, there are fifty Papists who become Protestants. Your people begin to feel that they have permitted their mercenary priests to think for them long enough; they now commence thinking for themselves. And I am pleased to inform you that even Kirwan's Letters have been eagerly sought for by many of them, and have been blessed to the hopeful conversion of not a few. You say the Catholic religion is now looked upon with less disfavor than formerly. I am persuaded, sir, that you mistake upon this subject. Controversy has assumed a kinder tone, and efforts are put forth in a more quiet and Christian way than formerly; but the mind of the world and its piety were never more intently engaged for the overthrow of Popery, than at the present hour. You, sir, are regarded as at the head of a political party—you are regarded as carrying the vote of the papal Irish in your pocket. Papists, *even here*, are regarded as so wedded to the pope, as to be willing to cast their vote for the party that praises him loudest. These, sir, are the reasons why you misread the attentions which are paid yourself, and the eulogies which are pronounced on the pope. Some of the very men that flatter you in public, and that applaud the pope in the Tabernacle, contemn you in their hearts, and pray at their family altars that popish superstition may come to a perpetual end. And you well know it all.

Yet, sir, there is an excitement on the public mind which will secure a reading for what you or I may say, kindly and intelligently, as to Popery or Protestantism. I have stated my objections to your church. It is a matter of public regret that you have not resolved to meet and obviate them. You have marked out, however, your own course; you have attempted to show the reasons why no Catholic should forsake his church, and why all Protestants should seek her communion as soon as possible. It will be my pleasure to follow you step by step, and to show the utter truthlessness of every argument you have adduced to show that yours is the one, holy, catholic and apostolical church, out of whose communion there is no salvation. This no man has ever yet succeeded in doing. Can you hope to be successful where others, more learned, more acute, and less burdened with duties, have failed?

My objections to your church are before the world. They stand there, abused, but unanswered. This is one point gained. It will be gaining another if I can show the baselessness of every argument you use to bind your people to it, and to induce others to enter it. To do this will be my object in the following letters.

Yours,

KIRWAN.

LETTER II.

Bishop Hughes' letters characterized—Coolness of their statements—Their argument one enforcing despotism—The principle that the Bible has no authority but what the church gives it, and that it must be undersood as the church interprets it, examined.

MY DEAR SIR,—I now proceed to the examination of the letters which you have addressed to a "Dear Reader," and of which mine to you have been the occasion. I have taken the stand point outside your church which you requested your "Reader" to take, and there I have considered and inwardly digested them. My views in reference to them I will now frankly and candidly give to you and to the public. And if a word or sentiment shall escape me, not essential to my main object, that will give you pain, I beg you to charge it to the account of that frailty of our common natures from which alas! neither Peter nor his successors were, or are exempt.

These letters give the old statement about the papal being the only true church, and in the old way; a statement which has been better made very many times. There is an utter absence from it of freshness; it is a mere distillation from other minds wonderfully weakened in the process. Out of the old beaten track of Christ appointing apostles and making Peter their pope—of giving to them, and especially to him, the keys of the kingdom, you seem unable to take a step. And you present the argument, if it can be so called, in the weakest and dullest form that I have yet seen it. How to account for this—whether on the ground of an over-estimate of your talents, or that you are reasoning against your own interior convictions—I know not. Although comparatively unknown, and with but little general reputation at stake, I would not be the author of them for your crook, keys, and mitre.

A remarkable feature of these letters is the coolness and confidence with which their statements are made. These statements have been logically and theologically refuted very many times; and yet you reproduce them with as much composure as if they were the utterance of the divine Spirit; as if they were not the merest, and some of them the most foolish assumptions. The argument of assertion is one in which your church is very powerful, because with a certain order of mind it is so potent. With many it is sufficient to know that the pope, the bishop or the priest says so. And it is difficult to conjecture what those may not say who affirm that they can change a little wafer made of flour into the real body and blood of Christ. But you, sir, should know that you live not in the age of Thomas Aquinas, and that you are read by increasing multitudes in your own church, with whom assertion is simply assertion.

The argument of these letters is one maintaining and enforcing ecclesiastical despotism. Christ appointed apostles—over the twelve he placed Peter as pope—to these and their successors he gave the government of the church in all ages and countries; —and the power of the keys to admit or to exclude, to bind or to loose, as they might deem meet. And all who submit not to this external arrangement which you call "the body of the Church," must be both to God and to the church as heathen and publicans. If this argument is true then there is not a man on earth who can be saved, however he may submit to the yoke of Christ, unless, in addition, he puts on the yoke of the pope. And yet the gospel is called a "law of liberty;" and the generous and warm-hearted Peter, who, although according to your showing the first pope, yet wore no shackles, declares, "of a truth I perceive that God is no respecter of persons, but in every nation he that feareth him, and worketh righteousness, is accepted of him." Sir, the monstrous conclusion to which it leads proves your argument to be a monstrous one; and that argument is put forth at a time when the divine right of kings and priests to enslave the nations, civilly and spiritually, is passing away like the foam upon the waters, before the indignant scorn of the world! The fate of the doctrine of divine right to hold in bondage the bodies and souls of men, as held by kings and papal priests, reached this country about the commencement of last Lent, when your letters died. I have sometimes thought that a coroner's jury empanneled to investigate the cause of the death of your letters would render the following verdict: "Died because of the gracious visitation of Almighty God upon the doctrine of divine right, as held by kings and popes and bishops and other inferior clergy, which has recently taken place in Europe."

But I pass from the general impressions made by the perusal of your letters to the consideration of their statements. You will remember that my work is not to prove any thing save the utter truthlessness of your positions. Your numbered paragraphs are like stones in a pile, in contact, but without any logical arrangement or connection. I will cull from them your main principles, and will seek to show you that they are the merest papal assumptions. In doing this I will not confine myself to your arrangement, nor yet to your language or method of argumentation. I will even give to your principles the advantage of the better statement made of them by standard papal authors; as I truly believe that nothing is finally lost by fairness.

1. *You assert that the Bible has no authority save what your church gives it, and that it must be understood and received as your church interprets it.* And you flout private interpretation as the root of all

heresy, and of all evil. Although this is not among your first postulates, I select it as the first for examination, because of its fundamental importance. If I have no right to read, or interpret the Bible, or to deduce from a single passage of it a meaning differing from that which your church puts upon it, then controversy is ended. I am shut up either to return to holy mother or to go to hell. Now, sir, as by the grace of God I intend to do neither the one or the other, I will show you that the principle above asserted is a false assumption. To be sure it is not yours, nor Milner's, nor Hay's merely, it is asserted by the Council of Trent, and all are cursed who refuse to receive it.

The first question I wish to ask is, where is the authority you claim for your church, given her? Upon this point I must have proof beyond question. Do you assert the need of an infallible interpreter of the will of God? Such an one would be convenient;—but where is such need asserted?—where is such an interpreter appointed? If you point me to a passage of Scripture you admit my right of private interpretation, for I must exercise my judgment to decide whether it is or is not to the point. If you tell me that uniform tradition asserts the possession of this authority by the church, how do I know that your tradition is true? Your church has corrupted the written words;—hence I may infer, that if there is any such thing as unwritten tradition she has corrupted that also.

The Scriptures, you say (No. 10), owe to your church their character for authenticity and inspiration. How is this? The Old Testament was completed, and was in use hundreds of years before the coming of Christ;—the Evangelists and Apostles who wrote the New Testament were inspired so to do by the Holy Ghost. These things are capable of the fullest proof—nor would their proof be weakened a hair, if the whole papal church were swallowed up with the company of "Core." Why is the Bible more than any other ancient book indebted to your church for its character? Do we not prove the Apocryphal books uninspired which your church places in the Canon?—and with equal facility could we not prove the Epistles of Paul to be inspired if your church had taught otherwise? Do we not, with the utmost facility, show all your corruptions of Christianity and of the Scriptures, and separate the false from the true as easily as does the husbandman the chaff from the wheat?

The Scriptures, as we possess them, existed before the rise of your church—before a general council ever commenced—before a declaration was ever made by a council as to the canon of Scripture. Any such declaration must be founded on antecedent evidence. And unless such evidence existed previous to the declaration of it—the declaration itself is a falsehood. Let it then be granted that we have no evidence of the truth of Scripture save what the Church of Rome gives us, and the whole fabric of Christianity totters to its base. Are you prepared for this result? or would you rather sustain Popery than Christianity?

Truth is the great object proposed by God to our belief. Religious differs from other truth only in its superior importance. All truths in the universe are connected together, and make an harmonious whole. They strengthen and fortify each other. And as God proposes truth to our belief, he has endowed us with minds capable of examining the claims of all things soliciting our belief, and has surrounded us with motives ever impelling us to seek and to love the truth. We have in the works of God the evidences of his eternal power and Godhead—we have in his word the more full revelation of his will. And he has so formed us that we cannot believe without proof, and that we cannot reject with. At least I know of no way of doing otherwise save by turning Papist. Now why should the Bible be exempted from the general law which rules my acceptance of all truth? Whilst permitted to think for myself on all other subjects, why should I be forbidden to investigate the Scriptures for myself? Why bound up to believe them only as your church interprets them? Sir, there must be some priestly device at the bottom of all this. As reasonably might your church forbid me to believe any thing in astronomy, or in physical or moral philosophy, contrary to her teaching, as forbid me to receive the Bible save in the sense which she gives it. And you remember she sent Galileo to prison for teaching that the earth moves around the sun.

I must believe the Scriptures only in the sense of your church—"holy mother!" But who is she? where is her residence? You define her, in a controversy with a late distinguished divine, to be "the visible society of Christians, composed of the people who are taught and the pastors who teach, by virtue of a certain divine commission recorded in the 28th of Matthew, addressed to the Apostles and their legitimate successors until the end of the world." So that the people and their pastors constitute "holy mother church;" and "holy mother" is the rule of faith. So that "holy mother" is the rule of "holy mother;" that is, the venerable and fretful old lady wills as she wishes, and does as she wills! Has not this been very much so?

But *the people and their pastors* form the church, and the church is the rule of faith! And yet the people and their true pastors, those who daily labor among them, visiting their sick, and burying their dead, have nothing to do with the rule. The authoritative meaning of Scripture is declared by your bishops, and even of these not one in ten has any thing to do with it. What, for instance, have you to do with it? Practically it is in the hands of the pope and his cardinals. So that "*holy mother*," the rule of faith, is made up of a few *holy fathers*, many of whom as to sense are the merest drivelers, and as to morals the merest debauchees! Now, sir, if

I go to these *holy fathers*, who, individually, are men, but who, unitedly, are "*holy mother*," for the sense of Scripture, must not my religion be based upon man? And from building upon such men I am compelled to cry out in the language of the Litany, "may the good Lord deliver me."

But admitting, for the sake of the argument, that I am bound to receive the Scriptures as your church interprets them, then will you answer me a few questions? How am I to obtain her sense of them? On the greater part of the Scriptures she has given forth no binding interpretation. At what period of the life of holy mother am I most likely to get a true interpretation? Is it when she was Arian with Pope Liberius? or when she was pagan with Marcellinus? or when she was Pelagian with Pope Clement XI? or when she was infidel with Leo X? or when strumpets were her waiting maids with John XII and Alexander? or is it when she was drunk with the blood of the martyrs? or when rival popes were tearing out each other's bowels? or is it when in the height of her charity she was thundering her curses from Trent against all who refused to say Amen to her decisions? These, sir, are very important questions to be answered, as I may be Arian, Pelagian, or infidel, a Calvinist, or an Arminian, according to the time I seek from holy mother her interpretations of the word of God. Perhaps my reverence for the venerable old lady, now in her wrinkles and dotage, might be greater than it is, were it not for my sense of her dissolute and change-ful life.

But I find I have finished a letter without finishing my analysis of the principle under examination. I will resume it in my next.

Yours, &c.,

KIRWAN.

LETTER III.

Examination of Church interpretation continued.

MY DEAR SIR,—In my last letter I commenced, without concluding, an examination of the principle, *that the Bible has no authority save what your church gives it, and that it must be understood and received as your church interprets it.* Upon this principle, sufficiently disproved by the considerations already presented, I have a few things more to say.

I must receive the Scriptures in the sense and meaning which your church gives them! God is *my* father, and Jesus Christ is *my* Saviour as well as yours. His word is a revelation of his will to *me* as well as to you, or as to any body of men upon earth. "God at sundry times and in divers manners spake in times past to the prophets, and in these last days he has spoken to us by his Son." So that notwithstanding the puerile distinction, unworthy of a man of sense, you make (No. 40), God does speak to *me* through the prophets, and his Son, in his word. And yet I must not hear him,—nor consider his sayings as possessing any authority or meaning, until holy mother gives his sayings to me authority and meaning! That is, I must hear God only when he uses the lips of holy mother; lips which have blistered under the curses which she has been pronouncing against me for ages! Holy mother, sir, in the bloom of her youth, and in the maturity of her years, "lived deliciously and courted kings to her couch." But hers has been a dissolute life. She has made the earth drunk with the wine of her fornication. And although in her wrinkles and dotage, you now tell me that I can hear God only through her; and that I must bow my ear to the stream of her fetid breath, and at the risk of all your curses, learn God's will only as she expounds it! If such a claim, calmly put forth, is not a proof of dotage, what can be? Bishop Hughes, how old are you?

But why bind me to receive the Scriptures only in the sense which your church gives them? How can I know that she gives them a correct sense? Or must I take this for granted? The popes are admitted to be infallible. So are the bishops; and so are general councils. Pope has contradicted pope—bishop, bishop—and council, council. How then can I confide in their interpretation of Scripture? How can I be infallibly assured that any other man, or body of men, is infallibly qualified to guide me into the meaning of the Scriptures? If I, Kirwan, reject my own prayerfully received sense of Scripture for yours, John Hughes, then are not you above the Scriptures to me? And do not I virtually reject what God says, for what you say, who can now and then turn a sharp corner and leave the truth behind you? And if this is not infidelity, what is it?

But to this you reply that I must not look to your interpretation, but, as says the creed of Pius IV, to "the unanimous consent of the Fathers." But here again, the "private reasoner" has some important questions to ask. Who are the Fathers? Where or with whom do they begin or end? This is an unsettled question. Were they not uninspired men and fallible? This is admitted. Origen, among other errors, taught Universalism. Augustine retracted his errors. Tertullian was a Montanist. And can fallible men make an infallible rule?

Besides, the early fathers wrote but little in the way of Scriptural interpretation. If any thing, we have scarcely any thing from the Fathers before the middle of the second century; and but little, save fragments, of the first three centuries, and these corrupted. And what we have from those early times serves no purpose in settling the points in controversy. They differed widely among themselves,—some of them condemn your Apocrypha—some of them your absurd doctrine of transubstantiation. And yet whilst these fathers were fallible, and differed among themselves—whilst they pointedly condemn in some things the teachings of your church, and wrote but little in the way of Scriptural interpretation, yet we must receive the Scriptures "according to the unanimous consent of the Fathers." Is not this prepos-

terous? Have you not excommunicate your common sense and reason?

But, for the sake of the argument, let us admit that these erring and contending fathers were unanimous in their support of the distinguishing doctrines of your church. What, then, does this avail? If unanimous in teaching what the Scriptures do not, their teaching cannot be received; if in what the Scriptures do teach, we receive that without them. Nor is unity any evidence of truth, in itself. Men in multitudes have been united, for ages, in supporting a lie. And union is in the inverse ratio of knowledge. The more perfect the ignorance, other things being equal, the more perfect the union. When the blind lead the blind they cling very close together. Individuals in full vision often select different roads to the same place; but the blind crowd along the same road, and cling to one another like swarming bees, even on the brink of the precipice. Hence the proverb, "if the blind lead the blind both will fall into the ditch." And if the successors of Moses, who sat in his seat, and boasted that they were his ecclesiastical descendants, were blind leaders of the blind; may it not be possible that the same may be the case as to the descendants of Peter? Your letters, now before me, give the plainest evidence that the eyes of your mind stand in great need of couching. O that you might apply to them the eye-salve spoken of in Revelation.

But you reply, this is forbidden by the fact that

your bishops are the descendants of Peter, and that they have the promise of divine guidance. But they are no more the descendants of Peter, than were the Jewish priests the descendants of Moses and Aaron. So that reasoning from the one to the other this plea avails nothing. "We be Abraham's seed," said the Jews. "If ye were Abraham's children ye would do his works," replied the Saviour. "We be Moses' disciples," cried the Pharisees. "Had ye believed Moses ye would have believed me," says Christ. And it is surprising that a man, like you, professing to be a master in Israel, and a chief pastor in the church of God, could for a moment lose sight of the palpable truth that the true evidence of apostolical succession is apostolical faith and practice. In your fourth letter, (No. 41,) you speak of Joanna Southcote, Joe Smith, and father Miller with a sneer; but, sir, the most absurd absurdity of Joe Smith was clever sense when compared with your principle of making fallible men infallible expounders of God's revealed will, and sending all to perdition who do not receive their unanimous consent as its true meaning, when no such consent was ever given, or can be found! Sir, Joe Smith was much more of a pope than you imagine. He damned, as unblushingly as you or holy mother, all that did not deem him and his cardinals infallible, and that rejected his Mormon tradition. And if as a "private reasoner" I were compelled to select Joe Smith or John Hughes as my chief Rabbi, notwithstanding "the sympathies of my Irish nature," I would not long hesitate between them. I have no great relish for the nonsense of either of you, but I could swallow his with far less difficulty and grimace, than I could yours; and I would sooner get through. My throat would not have to be stretched, almost to the cracking of its skin, every day of my life, for the purpose of taking down some monstrous absurdity.

But you plead the need of receiving the Scriptures in the sense given them by your church, to save the church and the world from the divisions and schisms which are the necessary result of private interpretation. It is to be regretted, on the whole, that those who reject church interpretation are so much divided among themselves. But it is difficult to form any machinery, however perfect, without some friction. Like all other good things, the right of private judgment has been abused. But what, sir, has been so awfully abused as the doctrines of church interpretation and sacramental grace, two of the prime doctrines of holy mother? Diversity of opinion is necessarily connected with the exercise of the right of private judgment; as God has no more made minds to think alike than he has faces to look alike, or temperaments to act alike. God and nature abhor dead levels. Uniformity with diversity seems to be the great law of Jehovah. And whether to surrender our right of private judgment in religious things for the sake of a level uniformity, or to retain it with the variety of opinions which may spring from it, is the question which here divides the Papist from the Protestant. To my mind it is like the question whether we shall have a free open sea, with its ceaseless sounding, its ever heaving bosom, and its billows occasionally rolled to the sky by the tempest, or a sea bound in fetters, with an unruffled bosom, stagnating by day and by night, and sending over earth and air its putrid exhalations.

Whilst I deplore the divisions among Protestants and feel that they are unnecessary, evincing less forbearance than passion, yet, sir, does holy mother exclude them from her pale by her stringent rule of church interpretation ? Has she had no schisms in her bosom ? Among her numerous progeny have there been no Mother Ann Lees, no Joe Smiths, no Father Millers ? Perhaps, sir, you forget that the fathers of Protestantism have contended, in every age, with all forms of fanaticism ; and have used all weapons against them, save those potent ones of your church, fire and faggot. Has your church done so ? Has not your priesthood, in every age, fostered fanaticism and absurdity ? Liberius patronized Arianism, a branch of Socinianism. Montanus, more than a rival for Swedenborg. was patronized by his cotemporary pope. And the fanaticism of Mother Lee, and of Joanna, go out as do the stars amid the effulgence of the sun, when compared with the fanaticism of Beata of Cuenza, who, teaching that her body was transubstantiated into our Lord's body, was conducted with processions to the churches where she was adored, as you now adore the host; or with that of Clara of Madrid, who claimed, and was allowed, to be a prophetess; or of sister Nativité, who saw on one occasion in the hands of the officiating priest, at the consecration of the wafer, a little child, living and clothed with light. The child, eager to be eaten, spoke with an infantile voice and desired to be swallowed! And you, sir, a bishop in a church whose history is crowded with the feats of such fanatics, and whose bishops and popes have been their patrons, will quote against Protestants the examples of a few fanatics that we have ever opposed, to prove to us the mischief of interpreting the Bible for ourselves! Bishop Hughes! Bishop Hughes!! O Bishop Hughes!!!

Nor is this all. You dwell upon our divisions and schisms as proof to demonstration against our private interpretation; forgetting that if strong against us, it is equally strong against church interpretation. Have you never read of, or have you conveniently forgotten, the western schism which rent the bosom of holy mother? Have you forgotten the feuds between the Jansenists and the Jesuits, and those caused by the Augustines and the Dominicans? Have you never read of the Scotists and Thomists—of the war about the immaculate conception of the Virgin Mary between the Franciscans and Dominicans—of the feud between the Franciscans and Pope John? Through every century of her existence the bosom of holy mother has been rent by internal feuds such as have never cursed the Protestant world. And at this very hour her bosom is like the bowels of Etna when on the eve of an eruption.

Sir, it would have been well for you had you made yourself better acquainted with the annals of Popery and Protestantism, to use your own classical and dignified language, "before you had launched your shallow bark on the ocean of ecclesiastical history."

I will recur again to this subject in my next.

Yours, &c.

KIRWAN.

LETTER IV.

Examination of Church interpretation continued—Its destructive consequences—It is a monstrous assumption.

My dear Sir,—At the close of my last letter I was considering your argument for church interpretation drawn from the divisions and schisms which prevail among Protestants. Although I have shown that the argument against private, is equally strong against church interpretation, I have a few things more to say in reference to it. As it is your *taking* argument with weak minds, it requires more attention than its merits deserve. Like almost all *taking* arguments, it is a weak one.

I have already shown how grievously, in every age, your church has been rent by schism, and disgraced by fanaticism. I would now ask why the distinction you set up between *doctrine*, and *discipline* and *morals?* The church is infallible in doctrine, but not in discipline or morals! And when we compare the things in which she is infallible, with those in which she is not, the latter far outnumber the former. Now why the distinction? The few things in which you agree are called doctrine; and the many in which you do not agree are called discipline and morals! So that the distinction is made to excuse the infinite diversity of opinion that exists among you; and also to excuse the shocking enormities committed by your church as mere matters of discipline and morals! And yet, singular to state, your church pronounces equally heavy curses against those who reject her discipline and morals, on which she has made no infallible decision, as against those who reject her doctrines, on which she has!

Now, sir, if the above distinction between doctrines, and discipline and morals, is a true one, which I utterly deny;—if a people may be considered a unity who unite in a few radical doctrines however they may disagree on things pertaining to discipline and morals, I am prepared to show that the unity of the Protestant world far, very far surpasses that of the Papal. The things in which we agree are more numerous and more important than are your infallible doctrines, and the things in which we disagree are less numerous and less important than are your matters of discipline and morals. And yet you come near waxing eloquent, and becoming interesting on our diversity, when contrasted with your unity! But, I suppose we must excuse you on the ground that you are writing for Roman Catholics, who, poor creatures, are excluded from the ranks of "private" or public "reasoners.' Nothing saves this argument from derision, but my unwillingness to offend against decorum.

"The church gives authority and meaning to the Scriptures, and we must receive them as the church interprets them." The Scriptures, the Apocrypha, the unanimous consent of the fathers, the sacred canons, the decisions of councils, and oral traditions, form your rule of faith. And as these, like the Bible, which you seem as much disposed to ridicule as to eulogize, are made up of paper, types and ink, and are silent when you ask them any questions, they need a living interpreter. And to avail, he or she must be infallible. This living, infallible interpreter is your church. That is, as I have already shown, the church is the rule of the church. To him who is infallible all faith and practice are equally true. The truth of principles changes as he changes. Infallibility prevents the correction of error—makes principles however opposite equally true—obliges the infallible one when he goes wrong to defend the wrong, and to stay wrong for ever. Thus, as your church has been on all sides of almost all questions, because infallible, she makes the opposite sides equally true; and thus lays the axe at the root of all true principles and of all true morals. And the facts in the case prove the truth of my inference. What truer sons of your church has the earth ever borne than the Jesuits? And what class of men have so undermined the foundations of all true principles and morals! Have you read Pascal's Letters? So that it may be laid down as a principle equally true of men and of nations, the more entirely papal, the more entire the absence of sound principles and sound morals. The maximum of the one is always in connection with the minimum of the other.

I think, sir, that if you do not, all "private reasoners" will agree that I have shown your principle, that "the Bible has no authority but what your church gives it, and that we must receive it as your church interprets it," is the merest assumption. It is a principle unworthy of you as a man; more unworthy of you as a minister of the God of truth; and deserving only the scornful rejection of all intelligent and thinking men. But as the destinies of this ruined world and of the true church of God are bound up in the principle, let us look at its effects when carried out.

"The interpretation of the church;" this is your great principle, and your catholicon for all divisions and heresies. The Jewish church was infallible, as your chief writers assert. And the Jewish people were bound to receive the Scriptures as interpreted by those who sat in Moses' seat. And yet this infallible church, by its infallible teachers, put to death the Lord of glory. Jesus Christ, then, fell a victim to the very principle which you assert—the principle of church interpretation. And how many of the most devoted followers of Jesus Christ have fallen victims to the same principle, we are not to know until the day of final revealing.

Church interpretation is exclusive of private judgment. If true it would have forever prevented the erection of the Christian church. It would have bound all Jews to remain Jews forever, and all other men to become Jews in belief, in order to enter heaven. Like your church the Jewish made void the law of God by traditions. Their traditions and church interpretation of the Scriptures were all against Jesus Christ; how then, on your principles, could the foundations of the church of Christ be laid? They never could be. How were they laid? By those who rejected church interpretation, and who for themselves examined the Scriptures, and considered the evidences which proved to them that Jesus was the Messiah. You, sir, as a minister, owe your standing in the church of Jesus Christ to the rejection of the very principle which you assert, and, with so much flimsy sophistry, enforce; and to the adoption of the principle of private interpretation which, in seeking to vilify, you only expose yourself to scorn. Your argument is contemptible, and makes you ridiculous.

Nor is this all. If we carry out your principles how can you expect us to return to your church? Let me make the case my own to give point and directness to what I say. I am an unbeliever, but sincerely inquiring after the true church; and I go to your residence to have my inquiries answered. You state to me the marks of the true church, beginning with that of *unity*, and quote some Scripture in confirmation. But what must I do? for I am forbidden the exercise of my private judgment. If I say the mark is a true one, and is based on Scripture, that is a private judgment which I have no right to exercise; if I deny it, and the relevancy of the texts quoted, it is again a rejection of your principle. You pass on to the next mark, *sanctity*, and dwell upon your holiness of doctrine. To be satisfied of this being a true mark, I must compare your doctrines with those of the Scriptures; if I come to the conclusion the mark is a true one, I reject your rule; if to the opposite conclusion I yet reject it. Our conversation ends, and I retire either impressed by your arguments, or bewildered by your sophistry. In a few days I return, saying, "Well, Bishop Hughes. I have deeply considered your statements, and I have concluded that they are true, and that yours is the true church; and I wish to connect myself with it." Would you receive me? Gladly. And yet by receiving me you deny the truth of your own rule, and admit that a man on his private judgment can "make an act of faith." If converts cannot be made in this way to Popery how can they be? If made in this way where is the force or the truth of your denunciations of private judgment? If men have no right to read or to judge of the Scriptures for themselves—no right to form an opinion as to the clashing claims for the true church, why the series of letters before me, in which bold assertion, a little truth, much sophistry, perverted texts of Scripture, and no little arrogance, are mixed and mingled together to prove that yours is the true church, and to induce all to flee to her fold who wish to escape perdition ? Sir, your doctrine is a suicidal one ; your church cannot live with it, nor can it live without. It is gotten up for babes in intellect, and not for men.

But let us admit the full truth of the doctrine, and that it is binding on every mortal ; what follows ? I must give up my Bible and lock up my private judgment. Wishing to know what meaning the church gives John 5 : 39, I apply to my neighboring priest. But he has not read the fathers, nor the canon law, nor the decrees of councils, nor the bulls of the pope, nor the Scriptures. He applies to you his bishop ; nor have you read them. You apply to the archbishop ; nor has he read them. He applies to the cardinals ; nor have they read them. They apply to the pope ; nor has he read them. I here venture the assertion that there is not a living man who has read your rule of faith. How can I know then what the church teaches ? Even if her teachings were harmonious, there is no knowing. But, for the argument, I grant that the pope and his cardinals, who virtually compose "holy mother," do know the rule. They tell the archbishop, he tells you, you tell the priest, and the priest tells me. And however my common sense revolts against it, I must receive it, as a good son of the church !

See hen the position to which your doctrine reduces every thinking and thoughtless man. It brings us all on our knees before your priests, multitudes of whom are as unprincipled and wicked as they are ignorant; deprives us of the right of private judgment, and compels us to open our minds and souls to whatever nonsense, concocted in Italy, they might see fit to ladle into them.

These, sir, are the considerations which prove the principle I have been considering not only a mere but a monstrous assumption; a principle which, whether true or untrue, is equally fatal to the claims of your church. I deeply regret that any clever son of old Ireland, after breathing so long the air of freedom, should lend himself to the support of such a monstrous principle. The logical power which you display in its support gives you high claims to the chair of logic in the university of Heliopolis!

How pleasant it is to turn from such a rule to the simple and pure word of God, given to be a lamp to our feet and a light to our paths. If with that lamp, we wander from the way, the fault is in ourselves. It is not because of the obscurity with which God has revealed his will, but because our foolish minds are darkened by reason of sin. But I must not forget that my only object is to show the utter fallacy of your principles.

Yours,

KIRWAN.

LETTER V.

The Papal Church theory—A mistake in selecting Peter for the tiara—The prayer of Christ for Peter realized, for him and all his successors—The question, Was Peter pope? examined.

MY DEAR SIR,—In my last letter I concluded my analysis of the principle you assert, that the Bible has no authority save what your church gives it, and that it must be understood and received as your church interprets it. A principle more untrue, more absurd, more suicidal, has never been asserted. It cannot be more absurd, but it is infinitely more dangerous, than your doctrine of transubstantiation. Although the refutation of that principle saps the foundation of all that you have written, yet there are other principles mixed up with your postulates that require notice. Among these is *the principle involved in your theory of the church.* As the paragraph which you mark 5, contains the great outline of your church theory, I will here quote it entire.

"5. But *twelve* Apostles, invested with *equal* authority, might disturb the order and defeat the object, which their Lord had appointed them to establish and secure. *His* kingdom was to be *one;* united in itself. *His* sheep were to be comprised in '*one fold*,' under '*one shepherd*,' and not under *twelve*. Accordingly, out of the twelve, being all Apostles, and as such equal in dignity and authority, He selected *one*, Peter; and in addition to the Apostleship, which he enjoyed like the others, conferred on him *special*, *singular*, and *individual* prerogative and power, which had not been conferred on the other eleven, either singularly or collectively; and, as our Lord had said many things to the multitude, at large, and some things to the Apostles alone, so, also, He addressed many instructions to the Apostles as such, *including Peter*, and *some things* to *Peter alone*, in which the others had no *direct* lot or part. Satan, he said, desired them (all), that he might sift them as wheat, but He prayed for Peter, that *his* faith might not fail; and that he, being once converted, should confirm his brethren. The efficacy of this prayer of the Man-God, has been realized in His church, from the days of Cephas himself, through the whole line of his successors, down to the exercise of the *chief Apostleship*, in our own times, by the great and illustrious Pius IX."

The great papal idea here asserted is the placing of Peter over the other Apostles as their superior, and as the "Vicar of Christ," and as the head of the church, and the perpetuation of this office in his successors, down to the present day. Do you not know, sir, that these claims set up in behalf of Peter have been proven, very many times, to be without the shadow of a foundation? And yet you assert them as confidently as if they had never been questioned, and quote Scripture to prove them, just as if we had a right to form any opinion adverse to yours on the subject! Before attempting to show, what has been so often shown before, that poor Peter was never made pope, there are one or two ideas I wish to suggest just here.

Do you not think that your church made a mistake in selecting Peter for the tiara? Would you not have succeeded better with some of the other Apostles, one of the "sons of thunder," for instance? And how papal would be the idea,—a son of thunder, "thundering from the Vatican!" Would you not have succeeded with John better than with Peter? You could have urged in his behalf that he was the beloved disciple—that he was often in the bosom of his Lord—that Peter on a certain occasion sent him to ask of the Saviour a question which he feared to ask himself—that he did higher service to the church by his writings, which form so large a part of the New Testament—that he outran Peter, and reached first the sepulchre—that he outlived all the other Apostles! And this would save you all questions about John the beloved disciple, the inspired Apostle, the lovely evangelist, being subject to a successor of Peter who probably had never seen Christ, nor, perhaps, Peter. If John were your candidate you could not say so much about "this rock," nor about "the keys;" but then you would not be as pressed as now about "get thee behind me, Satan," about Peter's swearing so, and denying his Master. My opinion is, but I am a "private reasoner," that you would have succeeded better with John. I would advise you to correct tradition, *for I have no doubt she has erred,* and substitute John for Peter. You will find it a wonderful relief.

The use you make of the text you quote in the above paragraph strikes me very singularly. Satan desired the Apostles, as he once did Job, that he might sift them as wheat. Knowing Peter to be most in danger of them all, he prayed especially for him; and from this passage, whose only object is to show that poor Peter was more in danger of falling under the influence of the devil than any of his brethren, you deduce an argument for his supremacy! I have no doubt, if hard pressed, that like some astute critics of former days, you could find the history of the children of Israel in the Iliad of Homer! What bounds can confine the power of a man who can create God out of a wafer?

Consider well the following sentence in the above paragraph; "the efficacy of this prayer of the Man-God, has been realized in his church, from the days of Cephas himself, through the whole line of his successors . . . down to the great and illustrious Pius IX." Considering all things this is a most extraordinary assertion. That is, Peter's faith never failed; nor has the faith of a single pope from Peter to Pius! Notwithstanding the prayer of his Master, Satan sifted Peter. In the hour of severe trial his faith failed. When accused in the palace of Pilate of being one of the disciples, "he began to curse and to swear, saying, I know not the man." And is it in this way that the efficacy of that prayer "has been realized through the whole line of his successors?" And yet, sir, Peter, cursing and swearing, was an angel, in comparison with many in "the line of his successors." I know not how you could make an assertion more historically false; and the truth of which your own writers, yes, and John Hughes himself, deny.

But the question returns, Was Peter made pope, to exercise supreme authority in the church; and was the power thus conferred upon him hereditary, to descend to all his successors in the See of Rome? This is a doctrine, or principle, with which your church stands or falls. The pope is the centre of unity, and to be separated from him, according to your showing, is to be cast out among heathens and publicans. This principle, involving the existence of your church, and my salvation, I deny, and put you on the proof.

If called to prove this principle in a court of justice, how would you proceed? Would you call upon tradition to give her testimony? But tradition has been in the keeping of the pope; and this would be like calling upon the pope to testify to his own supremacy, which, in view of the power and emoluments of his office, I have no doubt he would be willing to do. But would his testimony be received? Would you invoke the aid of the Scriptures? But this would be giving up one of your fundamental principles; as the Scriptures to us have no sense but what the church, which is virtually the pope, gives them. This would be again calling on the pope to testify to his own supremacy, which could not be admitted. But supposing you admit the common sense meaning of the Scriptures to bear on the case, which every body not a Papist is willing to do, where would you commence?

Would you cite the very pertinent passage in Luke (xxii. 24—30), where the Saviour so sharply rebukes his disciples, because there was a strife amongst them as to which of them should be greatest? or that of Mark (ix. 34), where, again reproving them for their contention about pre-eminence, he says: "If any man desire to be the first, the same shall be last of all and servant of all." Would not the judge say, "Bishop Hughes, these texts are not to the point; for if Peter were placed over the disciples, why contention among them for pre-eminence? Would not Christ have settled the matter at once, and say, contend no more, I have made Peter your pope?"

Driven thence, would you next cite the passage in Ephesians (iv. 11), where Paul enumerates the various kinds of teachers which Christ on his ascension gave to the church, as apostles, prophets, evangelists, pastors, teachers for the perfecting of the saints,—and the parallel passage in 1 Corinthians (xii. 28)? Would not the judge again say,

"Bishop Hughes, these are not to the point as they say nothing about a pope, nor a word about the supremacy of Peter."

Foiled again here, would you next cite the passage (1 Cor. i. 12) which informs us of pastors in the church of Corinth, one claiming to be of Paul, another of Apollos, and another of Peter? and then would you turn to the passage in Galatians (ii. 14), where Paul most sharply rebukes Peter for his dissimulation? Would not the judge reply, "Bishop Hughes, what do you mean? If Peter were pope, why did he not excommunicate the parties of Paul and Apollos at Corinth, those early protestants against his supremacy? If he were pope, why for a moment permit Paul at Antioch to dispute his right to dissemble when circumstances required him so to do? These passages, sir, are against you, instead of proving the position you assert."

Foiled again, would you cite the passage in Acts (viii. 14), where the apostles in Jerusalem sent Peter and John to Samaria to assist in carrying on the good work there; and that other passage in the 15th chapter of Acts, where James declares the decision of the council at Jerusalem, called to consider some ceremonial questions started among the churches of the Gentiles by Judaizing teachers? The judge would again reply, "These passages are not to the point; for if Peter were pope, would he bear to be *sent* by those beneath him to Samaria? Would he permit James to preside in Jerusalem, at that first council, and to declare its will; duties which devolved on him by right of office? These passages, sir, are sadly against you."

You now, with some little excitement created by these repulses, quoté the passage in Matthew (xvi. 18, 19): "Thou art Peter, and upon this rock I build my church; I will give unto thee the keys of the kingdom of heaven." This you do with an air of assurance, feeling that you have trapped the judge at last. But he replies, being at once a Christian and a sound lawyer, "Bishop Hughes, these are disputed texts as to their true import; and the point that you wish to establish, being one of transcendent importance, should have something to sustain it besides texts of controverted meaning. You so explain this text as to make Peter the foundation of the church; but Peter himself denies this, by asserting that Christ is its foundation (1 Peter, 2d chap). Paul also denies it when he says that Christ Jesus is the only foundation that has been, or can be laid (1 Cor. iii. 11); and when he represents Jesus Christ himself as the chief corner-stone (Eph. ii. 20). And Jerome, Chrysostom, Origen, Cyril, Hilary, Augustine, make "the rock" to mean, not Peter, but the faith, or confession of Peter. And as to the gift of the keys, that avails you nothing as to the supremacy of Peter, for they were given equally to the other apostles as to him. And besides, I do not see what could be gained by placing the church upon Peter; as, for all interests concerned, it is better that it should be built upon Christ."

Thus repulsed on every hand, I hear you ask, in an excited tone, rather warm for a bishop, "If these evidences are rejected, what will your honor admit as bearing upon the point?" With the calmness becoming a judge, he replies, "Bishop Hughes, I want proof, beyond question, that Jesus Christ made Peter pope. I want clear proof of the fact that he ever exercised the power of the pope in any one case. I want proof that ever one of the apostles or any other contemporary ever referred to him, or applied to him as pope. And as your object is to prove the perpetuity of the popedom, if you prove that Peter was invested with supremacy over the other apostles, I want you then to prove that that supremacy was not to end with his death, but that it was to be held in fee for his successor for ever. When, sir, these points are proved, and not before, you may look for a decision in your favor. Have you proof as to these points?"

Looking upon a judge with disdain who thus requires you to make brick without straw, and to prove what so many ages have taken for granted, you collect your papers and make your exit.

Sir, your assertion of the supremacy of Cephas is the merest assumption, and I think you must see it to be so. You would not claim the possession of an acre of land in an Irish bog if you could advance no better claim to it than you put forth for the supremacy of Peter. But the end is not yet.

Yours,

KIRWAN.

LETTER VI.

Was Pete. pope ? examination continued—But two arguments that cannot be answered—Tillotson's opinion.

My dear Sir,—In my last letter I entered upon an examination of the claims of the pope to supremacy without concluding it. I showed you that in the testing of these claims, the testimony of tradition was inadmissible; and that the teaching, the facts, and the tenor of the New Testament, are directly in opposition to them. But as a man of spirit, greatly unwilling that a mere "private reasoner" should have even the appearance of victory over you, you appear again in court to prove, by other evidence, that Peter was clothed by Christ with supremacy, and that he was first pope of Rome. The judge having already decided against the testimony adduced to prove the first point, and having called for evidence which you cannot adduce, you address yourself to the second, to prove that Peter was the first pope of Rome. You state the point, and his honor calls for the testimony. And with an air of triumph you adduce the early records of the church, from its foundation to the fifth century, among which are the books of the New Testament. The judge says, "Well, Bishop Hughes, we will commence with these documents, and examine them in their order." The proposition is a fair one, and you consent.

"Mark," says the judge, "was a friend and follower of Peter. He wrote his gospel at Rome, about thirty years after the ascension of Christ. Some of the fathers even say that it was revised by Peter. Does he say any thing about Peter being pope of Rome?" You reply, "No, Mark is silent on the subject." So that document is laid aside.

"Here are Peter's own letters," says the judge, "written but a short time previous to his death, thirty years at least after his alleged investiture with the supremacy. Do *they* say any thing upon the subject?" "No," you reply, "it would not be modest in him to say any thing about the matter." So these are laid aside, the judge remarking in an under tone, "It would have been well if the successors of Peter had imitated his modesty, who, after being nearly forty years pope, in two letters to the churches says not a word about his supremacy."

"Next are the letters of Paul," says the judge, "written from Rome, and to the Romans; do they bear any testimony to the point to be proved? His letter to the Romans was written several years after Peter was made Pope there; does he say any thing about pope Peter? At the close of the letter he sends his affectionate salutations to upwards of twenty persons; does he mention pope Peter? When, according to your showing, Peter was in the plenitude of his power at Rome, Paul was taken there as a prisoner. Whilst there he wrote several of these epistles, is Peter alluded to in them as pope? is he named at all? If he was there, Bishop Hughes, how do you account for what Paul writes to Timothy (2d Tim. iv. 16), "At my first answer . . . . all men forsook me?" Does Peter play again, in the court of Cæsar, the part he played in the palace of Pilate? Could Paul be a prisoner in Rome for two or more years, and pope Peter never do him any kindness? Could he have done him any kindness, and yet Paul never speak of it to his friends? How is all this?"

Vexed to the quick by these questions, for even bishops have feelings, and plainly perceiving that his honor is a "private reasoner," you reply, "we will lay aside, if you please, those documents which form the New Testament, and pass on to the next in order. They have always been wrested by 'private reasoners' to their own destruction, who are incapable of 'making an act of faith.'" "But before we lay them aside," says the judge, "do you admit, bishop, that they give no testimony to the point before the court?" You give a reluctant assent. He again asks, "How do you account for the fact that they give no testimony, considering the peculiar circumstances under which they were written?" You bite your lips, but are speechless.

After waiting a few minutes for a reply, the judge says, "We will proceed to the next document; what is it? what does it say?" "Here," you say, "is Jerome, who says that Peter went to Rome in the second year of Claudius, and was bishop there twenty-five years." "But," says the judge, "Jerome wrote about the year 400, and how did he know? where did he get the fact? In the 12th year of Claudius, Paul went to Jerusalem and found Peter there. Did he run away from Rome? Do popes now go from Rome to Jerusalem? or was he like some bishops in our day, who love the fleece more than the flock, a non-resident? In the reign of Nero, who succeeded Claudius, Paul went to Rome, and found the people there quite uninformed as to the faith of Christ (Acts xxviii. 17–24). If Peter was pope there for so many years previous, what was he about? Besides, the apostles were ministers at large; their duty was, not to abide in any city, not to demit their general for a local authority, but to go into all the earth, and preach the gospel to every creature. So that if these documents are true, they show that Peter, at least, was disobedient to the ascending command of his Lord, by locating himself at Rome, instead of laboring to extend the gospel to every creature. So that if these papers are true, and if they establish the point you press so earnestly, they will simply prove the unfaithfulness of Peter. If not true, your cause is lost; if true, Peter was a disobedient apostle, and ought to be condemned, instead of being followed and eulogized, for seeking his own ease instead of obeying his Master's command."

As the judge, seeking only the truth, places you in this sad dilemma, I see your Irish heart swelling with emotions. You seize your crook and your keys, and glance a wrathful look at the "private reasoner," so unfit to wear the ermine. But your sober second thoughts return, and you ask, with a tone of smothered indignation, "What proof does your honor want that Peter was bishop of Rome? What proof will you admit that the popes of our church are his true successors?"

His honor replies calmly but decidedly, "Bishop Hughes, the point you wish to prove is one of vital importance. It is the hinge upon which many grave questions turn, which deeply concern the destinies of our race. So you and I believe. To prove it I demand of you, not old wives' fables, but testimony so clear and direct, as to place it beyond a doubt. As to his being bishop of Rome, or being ever at Rome, the Scriptures are silent; and that they are silent, to you must be very embarrassing. And not only so, but upon this vital point the apostolic men who conversed with the apostles are equally silent as the Scriptures. Clemens, Barnabas, Hermas, Ignatius, Polycarp, say not a word upon the subject. At about the close of the second century Irenæus records it as a tradition received from one Papias, and is followed by your other authorities. But who Papias was, whilst there are various conjectures, nobody knows. And Eusebius speaks of the matter as a doubtful tradition. Here, sir, is the amount of your testimony; it resolves itself into the truth or falsehood of a prattling Papias, who told Irenæus that somebody told him that Peter was pope at Rome!"

"Now, sir, the evidence I require is, first, that he was ever at Rome; and secondly, that if there, he was pope of the universal church. And upon these points I will admit the testimony of the Scriptures, the apostles, or any competent cotemporary. If you have any such testimony produce it." You reply, "This is asking too much of an infallible church, whose unwritten tradition is of equal authority with the written word." His honor replies, "Bishop Hughes, it is asking a little too much to ask us to believe without evidence."

"You ask," continues the judge, "what evidence I will admit to prove that the popes are the successors of Peter? I want you, first, to prove that Peter was pope; if he was not he has no successors. If he was pope, I then wish you to explain why he was made pope, whilst he was set apart as the Apostle of the circumcision. You send him to the Gentiles whilst his peculiar vocation was to the Jews. I wish you also to explain, why make him pope of Rome, instead of Antioch, where we know he labored with great success; or instead of Jerusalem, where the Spirit was poured out, and where he preached with such remarkable power? Is it not probable that tradition has again misled you as to the location of the chair of Saint Peter."

"When you have proved and explained these things, then I wish you to tell by what body of men Peter was made pope at Rome, and how he was elected; for his successors must be so appointed and elected. I wish you to state how Peter was inaugurated at Rome, and what were the limits of his authority; for so his successors must be inaugurated and limited. I wish you to prove the duties devolved upon Peter, and his manner of discharging them; for such are the duties of his successors, and such must be their manner of discharging them. I wish you to prove the doctrines and morals preached and practised by Peter; as his successors must preach and practice the same doctrines and morals. Peter had a wife; have your popes? Peter called himself an elder; do your popes? Peter exercised no temporal power; is it so as to your popes? Peter devoted himself to preaching the gospel; do your popes? Peter was a man of no parade, though impulsive, and never asked any mortal to kiss his foot or his toe; is it so with your popes?"

Swelling with indignation you rise, and interrupting the judge, you exclaim, "Enough, enough; I see that your honor is a 'private reasoner,' incapable of 'making an act of faith,' and of course no better than a heathen or a publican. You are unfitted to sit upon such questions or to decide upon them." And collecting again your papers you leave the court, muttering in an under tone as you go, that if you had his Honor in Italy under the shadow of the sceptre of the illustrious Pius IX, you would teach him what was the true evidence a judge should require upon such points.

Thus, sir, in the form of a judicial investigation I have examined the testimony which your church adduces to prove that Peter was clothed by Jesus Christ with supremacy over the apostles—that he was the first pope of Rome—and that the popes of Rome are his legitimate successors. There is not a particle of reliable proof as to either of these positions—whilst the evidence is overwhelming that they are the merest and silliest papal assumptions. And yet upon assumptions based upon clouds which disappear before the light of investigation, you base the very existence and perpetuity of the church of God! It seems incredible that a man of sense, and an Irishman too, should suspend my salvation upon my church connection with men called popes, whose ignorance, and profligacy, and cruelty, and falsehood, have stamped their name with infamy—and tell me that my submission to God and his Son is of no avail unless I submit to these men, some of whom were devils in canonicals.

There are two items of proof in favor of the supremacy of Peter adduced by your church to which I have not alluded; I will state them to note my omission and for the information of our readers. The first is the passage in Luke (5 : 3–10), where Jesus entered into the ship of Peter, in preference to that of James and John, and taught the people out of it. In the view of Milner it is a strong proof of the supremacy of Peter ! ! The other is the story about Simon Magus, the magician. By his juggling miracles he made many followers, and greatly prejudiced the people against the gospel. He proclaimed that at Rome he was going to fly in the air; and Peter was there to oppose him. By the aid of the devil he absolutely got up in the air; but Peter knelt down and prayed so earnestly that the devil fled away and left poor Simon to shift for himself—he fell to the earth and broke both his legs. And the impressions of the apostle's knees upon the stones in Rome are shown to this day! These are the most unanswerable arguments upon the subject which I have seen. I could get round all the others, but these I give up!

"The pope's supremacy," said Tillotson, "is not only an indefensible, but also an impudent cause; there is not one tolerable argument for it, and there are a thousand invincible reasons against it."

I have now, sir, sapped two of your main principles; the supremacy of Peter and his successors, and that the Bible must be understood and received as your church interprets it. The taking away of these two principles brings your whole superstructure tumbling around you. Here I might leave you striving to escape from the falling masses; but "the sympathies of my Irish nature" compel me to say, the end is not yet.

Yours, KIRWAN.

LETTER VII.

Papal claim to infallibility examined, and refuted.

My dear Sir,—Although the *infallibility* of your church is involved and confuted in my previous letters; yet as you place so much stress upon it, and make it one of your fundamental principles, I have supposed it worthy of a separate and independent consideration. I will subject it to examination in the present letter.

In letter III, chap. 25, you say, "The Author of revelation identified Himself with his appointed witness, the church, in such a manner that the authority of the one is essentially implied and exercised in the authority of the other." That is, the church has the same authority and infallibility that Christ had. This is a plain, though bold assertion.

In letter V, chap. 54, you say, "Whether the words had ever been put on record or not (that is, whether the Scriptures had ever been written or not) she (the church) would have been equally in possession of that prerogative, namely, the vicarious authority to teach unerringly . . . until the end of the world, the doctrines of Christ . . . . What is the meaning of those passages if it be not to invest the official teachers of the Christian religion with the necessary portion of in-errancy, in other words, of infallibility, by its Divine author."

But there is no need of calling evidence to convict you of teaching the dogma, the infallibility of the papal church. It is one which your church has ever boldly and strenuously asserted; but the maximum of her bold and confident assertion is always in connection with the minimum of truth. To expose the utter truthlessness of the claim a few considerations will suffice.

1. How do you prove her infallibility? Tradition is inadmissible; because that has been, you say, in her keeping. It is, then, either a bribed, corrupted, or partial witness. The Scriptures, on your ground, are inadmissible, because the church must give them meaning; and a meaning which we are bound to receive. The church, you say, was before the Scriptures, and gives them credibility and meaning. Where is, then, the testimony to her infallibility? It is simply and only *her own assertion of it.*

2. But where is the seat of her infallibility? Is it in the pope? But this some popes deny, as Galasius, Innocent, Eugenius, Adrian, and Paul; whilst it is asserted by others. And those who assert it differ as to its extent. Whilst some popes deny their infallibility, the Jesuits say that "the pope is as unerring as the Son of God." Is this, sir, less than blasphemy, when you consider who some of your popes were?

Is it in a general council? Such is the system of the French school, and of some popes, and of some councils, as of Constance, Pisa, and Basil, which deposed some popes for high crimes. But in this the council of Lateran contradicts that of Basil.

Is it in a general council headed by the pope? This some positively affirm. But this is opposed by the two former parties, because denying the principle of each.

Is it in the church universal, consisting of pastors and people? So some assert, and among them, Panormitan and Mirandula. "Ecclesia universalis non potest errare," says Panormitan. This however is a small party opposing all, and opposed by all the others.

Now, sir, when you differ about the seat of infallibility so widely and bitterly, what can you expect better from a "private reasoner" than that he should ask you the impertinent questions, If your church is infallible, why does she not determine where her infallibility is located? What is her infallibility worth, if she never knows where to find it?

3. The infallibility of your church is too limited in extent. Because she has no tradition upon them, she gives no interpretation to many portions of the Scripture; and she forbids me interpreting them for myself! What are these portions worth? Might they not be as well omitted? She has no tradition

and *canno.* interpret them, and I *must* not! Here is a large portion of the Bible shut up from the world, as if never revealed! And yet Paul tells me that "*all Scripture* is profitable." Can that be an infallible church that knows nothing, and will permit me to know nothing, about a large portion of God's word?

Her infallibility covers only the field of *doctrine* and *morals*, and extends not to *discipline* and *opinions*. Now a list of the doctrines and morals on which she infallibly decides, and of the discipline and opinions on which she makes no such decision, and a narrative of her conduct in reference to them, would be a most curious paper. Will you favor the world with it, if you can? In matters of doctrine, in which your church is infallible, a man may believe as he desires, if he only clings to holy mother; but in matters of discipline and opinion, on which she has made no decision, if he acts out his honest convictions, he will have emptied on him the seven vials of papal wrath. For instance, the celibacy of the clergy, communion in one kind, are matters of discipline, and yet if you, Bishop Hughes, like Peter, should marry a wife—and a good one would be a great comfort to you, and would entitle you more fully to the title of bishop—or if after the example of Christ you should administer the supper in .he way it was instituted, you would soon be cast out as an apostate. Practically her infallible doctrines are minor matters, whilst those embraced under discipline and opinions are matters on which she has covered the earth with the blood and bones of murdered men. What is the judge worth who is unable to decide on all questions fairly brought before him arising under the laws?—and what is the infallibility of your church worth when unable to decide on the simplest questions as to discipline and opinions, and when she yet sends to perdition all those who deviate from her practice in these things? Paley tells us of a fish which, when pursued by its enemy, casts forth a liquid that muddles the water and blinds the eyes of its pursuer;—such is the object of your distinction between doctrines and discipline, but it has not the effect of screening your absurd dogma from being hunted down as an impertinent and wicked assumption.

4. If pope contradicted pope, council, council, if your church has taught and denied in one age what were denied and taught in another, as has been shown a thousand times, and as you may see in Barrow, Faber, and Edgar, where is her infallibility? But let me ask your attention to a few considerations bearing on the reasonableness of the thing.

Man in his best estate is fallible. The history of your own church teaches this beyond any other uninspired history extant. How can you make the fallible infallible? Can a whole be greater than its parts? Does the coming together of three hundred fallible men make them infallible?

If any of the bodies for which infallibility is claimed by your church were infallible, how account for their awful wickedness and grievous errors? If it inheres in the pope, were John, Benedict, and Alexander infallible; men born, as it would seem, to show how far human nature may sink in degeneracy? Were the popes raised to the chair of Peter by the courtezans Marozia and Theodora, infallible? Genebrand says that for one hundred and fifty years they were apostatical rather than Apostolical, and yet were they infallible? What say you, Bishop Hughes? Yes, or no.

But perhaps infallibility was in the councils. What does the noble Saint Gregory say of these? He compares their dissension and wrangling to the quarrels of geese and cranes gabbling and contending in confusion—and represents them as demoralizing instead of reforming. That of Byzantine, Nazianzen describes as a cabal of wretches fit for the house of correction. Cardinal Hugo thus addressed the council of Lyons on the withdrawal of the pope; "Friends," said he, "we have effected a work of great utility and charity in this city. When we came to Lyons we found only three or four brothels in it; we leave at our departure only one; but that extends from the eastern to the western gate of the city." For other details as to the councils, I refer you to Edgar, where papal authorities for these statements are fully cited. And yet were these councils, canonically convened, infallible? Does consecration by your church render a ruffian infallible? "The Holy Spirit," said Cardinal Mandrucio at Trent, "will not dwell in men who are vessels of impurity, and from such, therefore, no right judgment can be expected on questions of faith."

Can there be *doctrinal* without *moral* infallibility? Is not *moral* apostasy as culpable as *doctrinal?* Can there be infallibility without inspiration, without the special interposition of heaven in each case? Can it be transferred from pope to pope, from council to council? That your people may not err, does not your doctrine require infallible bishops to explain the decrees of popes or councils—and infallible priests to explain them to the people, and the people to be infallible so as not to misinterpret the priest? Where does the thing find an end? It is vain that councils send forth their decrees unless there is some infallible way of reaching their infallible meaning; and if their meaning is left to be developed by the "private reasoner," what better are you off than if you permitted him to read and to develop the meaning of the Scriptures for himself? Do you not know that Soto, a Dominican, and Vega, a Franciscan, gave contradictory interpretations to the decisions of the Council of Trent on Original Sin, the last council "that blessed the world by its orthodoxy, or cursed it by its nonsense?" Can it be possible that your claim for infallibility can have any thing to sustain it save "old wives' fables?"

The assertion of it would seem to argue either idiocy or insanity; or a pious knavery which would seek to entrap men by logical meshes woven out of assertion, falsehood, and imposture.

Nor, sir, have we yet reached the bottom of the absurdity. Your infallible church has set itself in opposition to the inspired word of God, and to correct its plainest principles. As I have illustrated this idea in some of my former letters, I can only now allude to it. The Bible makes God the only object of worship; you set men to worship the Virgin, the host, the cross, relics, pictures, and images. The Bible teaches that Jesus Christ is the only intercessor between God and man; you make as many intercessors as there are angels, apostles, martyrs, and saints, and send sinners to Mary more frequently than to her Son. The Bible teaches that nothing is sinful but a want of conformity to the law of God; you make the violation of your ceremonial laws sinful, and damnable, whilst the violation of the laws of God is a venial offence. The Bible teaches that to serve God aright we must be regenerated by the Spirit of God; you pronounce this a false and accursed doctrine, and teach that we are regenerated by baptism, and kept in a state of salvation by other sacraments and ceremonies which you have instituted. But I will not proceed in the sickening detail which proves, beyond doubt, that your infallible church has devised and is now seeking to propagate the merest caricature of Christianity ;—which demonstrates that there is the same difference between the religion of Jesus Christ and the religion of Rome, that there is between a sensible, well formed, well bred, well behaved gentleman, and a harlequin covered with gewgaws, seeking to amuse the people by his dress and his tricks.

Now, sir, in view of all these things, will you not bear with the infirmities of a "private reasoner," which compel him to pronounce your doctrine of infallibility the merest assumption, whose only object is to make serfs of the people, and tyrants of the priests? Instead of being infallible, your church is not credible; her testimony is not to be relied on, save when substantiated by other witnesses. This you will say is an awful proof of my apostasy. Be it so. Nor have I any idea that your faith in the doctrine is a whit stronger than mine. Cardinal Perron, you know, when dying, pronounced transubstantiation *a monster;* and some priests told Bishop Usher, that the chief part of their confession was *their infidelity* in the doctrines which they taught, and for which they mutually absolved one another. Is there nothing like this now going on in New-York? Have you never made, or heard such confessions?

Yours,

KIRWAN.

LETTER VIII.

The assertion that there are but two principles, authority and reason, for the determining of the meaning of Scripture, examined and confuted.

My dear Sir,—Having shown how utterly baseless and false are the main positions of your letters, and exposed their utter weakness and folly, as I fondly hope even to yourself, I might now let them rest. "The sympathies of my Irish nature" incline me to do so, as I fear your nervous system must be already sufficiently excited; but my love for the race surmounts those sympathies, and compels me to notice what you say about "private reasoners." And as it gives room for new and curious illustration, I will devote to it the present letter.

In paragraph 25, you say that there are but two principles, "authority and reason," by which we can truly determine the doctrines of revelation. "Authority" is the principle of the papist; "reason" is that of all not papists. The principle of "authority" leads into all truth; that of "reason" into all error. The reasoner cannot "make an act of faith"—the highest aspiration of his mind or heart is simply an "opinion." And, you say, "there is not a single expression of Holy Writ that can warrant the private reasoners of any age, whether past or present, to believe that they can be saved, so long as they trust to their own individual opinions for the attainment of the truth, and the means of spiritual life and participation in Christ." And all who now reject the authority of your church which now exercises the precise authority which Christ did whilst upon earth, you denounce as "private reasoners," incapable of faith, and as "necessarily out of the way which leads to eternal life." This, sir, is not speaking in Latin, as you do when you mumble masses; your English is more than usually plain here; and so will mine be, in examining the practical bearing of this cool assumption of your church to think for every body; of this cool exclusion from eternal life of all who will not permit you to think for them, and who dare to think for themselves.

The first idea suggested by all your dribble on the subject through half a dozen of letters is, that you seem to regret that God has endowed any body, save bishops and the inferior clergy, with the faculty of reason. The exercise of it on the subject of religion is denounced by you in every form as leading to schism, heresy, and hell. Now, sir, if the exercise of my reason is abstractedly so dangerous; if, in fact, when exercised, it leads to such awful results, how can you account for it that the Lord has endowed me with reason at all? On your principles would it not be better that I should have been born with a razor in my hand to cut my throat, than with reason in my mind which compels me *to think* on the subject of religion? Would it not be better for all *your* purposes that I should have no reason? And do you not daily find the simple facts that God has endowed man with reason, and with an awful bias to exercise it, greatly embarrassing to you? Do not these facts give rise to nearly all the difficulties with which you have to contend in the discharge of your apostolical duties? If men never turned "private reasoners," yours would be an easy and a *most lucrative* task!

With your theory fully carried out, and all "private reasoning" fully suppressed, and all "private reasoners" killed off, after the manner of the extermination of the Huguenots in France, by the authority of your church, earth would present to your rejoicing eyes an Arcadian scene such as the sun has not yet illumined. The people would be all sheep—yes, literal sheep—the pope would be the chief shepherd—you, John Hughes, and your other Right Reverend brethren would be his watch-dogs. If one of the poor sheep should ever think of straying from your stagnant waters after a clear rivulet flowing cool from under the rock at which to quench his thirst, if a bark would not terrify him back to his place, he would be soon torn to pieces as a warning to all the flock not to imitate his example. And then the chief shepherd and his dogs would have all the flock to themselves, from the wool to the fat, and from horn to hoof. And nothing prevents your getting out from such a purgatory of clashing opinions as that in which you are now placed, and rising up to such a paradise as I have here sketched, but that wicked and depraved disposition of men to question your authority, and to use their "private reason." Considering that this abominable abomination "private reason" thus excludes you from the paradise you desire, and shuts you up in a purgatory from which neither the efficacy of masses, nor "all the alms nor suffrages of the faithful" can deliver you, you have by no means sufficiently denounced it. There is no hope for you until it is put down! But I would advise you to strike at the fountain or cause of the evil, which is God, who endowed man with reason and knowledge—who has given him such a depraved disposition to use them, and who has commanded him to give "to every man a reason for the hope that is in him"—and who thus invites all men "Come now, let us reason together, saith the Lord." Go up, like a man, to the cause of the evil which you deplore, and you are at once in conflict with your Creator.

The next idea suggested by what you say about "private reason" is the utter inutility of the Bible. There are but two principles "authority and reason" by which we can know its meaning. Authority is in the hands of your church to be exercised as she wills: to read the Bible and reason about it leads to hell. Where, then, is the need of the Bible at all, save a few copies for the Bishops and inferior clergy which they may occasionally consult for the purpose of finding out chapter and verse of such texts as these: "Thou art Peter," "Confess your sins one to another." Sir, on your principles there is no need of it; and, hence, in purely Catholic countries you dispense with it. Do you remember how many Bibles Borrow could find in Spain? How many, think you, could be purchased in the bookstores of Rome? How many, think you, could be found among the peasantry of Munster and Connaught, who yet wear the yoke of your church? If all collected, I think they would not add materially to the weight of the bag in which you pack your vestments when going forth on some of your episcopal visitations. You talk about the Protestant translation as false—and as defective. But that is all in the air. The cause of your opposition to the Bible is bound up with your principle—"authority." What men read they will use their private reason about. And if the hidden man of your heart were known, it would be seen that you hate the circulation of the Bible as much as you hate Kirwan's Letters, as the one is the cause of the other. Sir, there is no possibility of sustaining "authority" versus "private reason," with a Bible circulated in whole or in part. So awfully fearful are you upon this point that many of your inferior clergy never see a copy of the Bible, lest they should become "private reasoners." Not long since I received a visit from a priest who acted as curate in Ireland,

and who told me that all of the Bible he ever saw, whilst in your church, were the small portions scattered, like angel's visits, through the Mass Book. Sir, your doctrine of "authority" supersedes the Bible; and its circulation leads to mortal sin because it makes men "private reasoners." What a pity the Bible was ever written! Would not this world of ours be a clover field for your priests, if the Bible, like your traditions, had only been left unwritten and unprinted? No wonder that the thunders of the Vatican are hurled at our Bible Societies, which are so awfully multiplying "private reasoners." But *mere* thunder, though noisy, is harmless.

There is yet another idea connected with what you say about "authority" and "reason," which in this country at least must strike one as singular. I have no doubt it will so strike yourself. When two clever men get into difficulty, they consent to have it fairly adjudicated, and to abide the decision of an impartial tribunal. If one declines such a reference, and insists on having it his own way, the fair inference would be that he was conscious of being in the wrong. Between the intelligent men of our race and your church there is a difficulty. Your church asserts the right of thinking for them, and damns them unless they permit her to do so; they deny that right. How is the question to be settled? They are an interested party, because their civil and spiritual freedom are involved; and so is your church, because if decided against her, she is ever afterwards deprived of "the alms and suffrages of the faithful." If your claim is true, they are slaves; if false, they are free, and your craft is ended. How is this matter to be decided? Your church replies, "With me is the authority to bind or to loose; it must be referred to me as the only competent authority." But they say, "No; you are an interested party—you have millions at stake—your character and standing before heaven and earth are at stake—your decision must be partial. But we will abide the decision of any tribunal save that which you set up." But your church says, "*No, you must abide by my decision or be damned.*" Sir, were men in conflict but for a dollar, this would wear knavery on the face of it; can it wear less when the points at issue are. whether your priests shall be despots, and the human race their pliant serfs?

There is yet another principle connected with your doctrine of "authority" and "private reason." The man that believes all you tell him "makes an act of faith;" but the poor "private reasoner" that goes to the Bible for himself can form only an "opinion" upon any subject. To illustrate. When you tell a poor papist who believes you, that Christ Jesus is co-equal with the Father, his belief of what you say is "an act of faith;" when I learn the same truth from the Bible and believe it, with me it is only an "opinion!" He believes on "authority" and I am a "private reasoner." His "act of faith" saves him; my "opinion" damns me; when his belief and mine are the same, with only this difference, he gets his "faith" from you; I, my "opinion" from the Bible! Sir, this is something more than driveling nonsense. It is contemptible blasphemy.

But let us try this scheme in its application to some texts and truths, that we may see how it works

"Bishop Hughes," says John Murphy, "what is the meaning of that text (James 5: 16), "Confess your faults *one to another*, and pray *for one another*." "Why, John," you reply, "it means confess your sins to the priest, and ask the priest to pray for you." John believes, and makes an act of faith. I, a little more cautious, look at the text, and thus reason about it. "One to another"—that looks very much like the priest confessing to me, if I confess to the priest, and I praying for the priest, if the priest prays for me. I look a little farther after "one another" or "one to another." I find in Heb. 3: 13, the following words, "exhort one another." Does this mean that the priest must exhort me, but not I the priest? Very well. I find the following words in Eph. 4: 32, "Be kind one to another, tender-hearted, forgiving one another." Does this mean that the priest must be kind and tender-hearted to me, and not I to the priest? that he must forgive me, but not I him? What say you, Bishop Hughes? Yet John Murphy believes you and makes an act of faith, and goes to confession and pays you and goes to heaven ; I, a "private reasoner" conclude you pervert the Scriptures to make a gain of godliness, confess my sins to God, and for my opinion go to hell !

John Murphy again asks, "Bishop, what is the meaning of Mat. 26 : 26, 27 ?" You reply, "Why, John, it means, that Christ transubstantiated the bread and the wine into his own body and blood, and that then he multiplied himself into twelve, and that then he gave himself to be eaten to each of the apostles, and after he was thus eaten, he was not eaten ; he was yet alive and spoke to them." With his eyes wonderfully dilated, he asks, "Bishop, is this done now ?" "O yes, John," you reply, "daily in the mass." He again asks, "Bishop, why not give the bread and the wine now to the people ?" "The reason, John, is," you reply, "that as the wafer is changed into the real body and blood of Christ, there is no need of it, for if we eat the whole body, we of course eat the blood with it." John is satisfied, makes an act of faith, and is saved ; I, looking a little farther into the Scriptures, soon conclude that the passage means, that the broken bread represented his body broken, and the wine in the cup his blood poured out. John Murphy for his act of faith is saved ; and I, poor Kirwan, for my opinion am damned ! !

Such, sir, is the way your rule works as to texts. Let us now see how it works as to some important truths.

John Murphy again approaches you and asks, "Bishop, how can I be saved?" "Why, John," you reply, "the church makes that very plain; you must be baptized, and go to mass, and perform penance—you must go regularly to confession; when dying you must receive extreme unction; then you must go to purgatory, from which you are to be delivered by the efficacy of masses, and by the alms and the suffrages of the faithful; and then you go to heaven." Amazed at the process, poor John makes an act of faith and is saved: I turn to the Scriptures, and preferring the word of God to yours, believe that "he that believeth in the Lord Jesus Christ shall be saved." John Murphy believes you, and is saved; I believe God and am damned. And so on to the end of the chapter. Why, Bishop Hughes, all this has not even the redeeming quality of being good nonsense: an article in whose production our countrymen are not usually deficient, even when their power as private reasoners is at low water mark.

Here, sir, I will close my review of your reasons for adherence to the Roman Catholic church as given in your ten letters to Dear Reader. Never were reasons more baseless, or weaker, presented to the human mind to justify either opinions or conduct. The way in which you state them obviously shows that you never examined them—that you received them as true as a good son of the church, without ever asking why or wherefore in reference to them. Your reception of them was obviously an act of faith, and not an opinion formed in the usual process of a private reasoner. And to ask me, or any sensible, thinking man, to believe in the Catholic church for the reasons presented in your letters, is on a par with asking me to believe that the little wafer made of flour, which you lay upon the tongue of a papist bowing before your altar, is transubstantiated by a miserably mumbled ceremony into the real body and blood of Christ.

Balaam's ass would never have had a name or a place on the page of history were it not for the whipping which his master gave him; and were it not for that whipping never would hairs from his tail have been preserved amid the sacred relics of Rome. Similar, I fear, will be the effect of this review in bringing up to public notice letters, which have neither sense, truth, wit, logic, or even "clever scurrility" to recommend them, and which if let alone might have reached the very depths of oblivion by the massive weight of their dullness.

But, sir, although through with your ten letters, the end is not yet.

Yours,

KIRWAN.

LETTER IX.

The Bishop s six letters to Kirwan, reviewed.

My dear Sir,—I wish in the present epistle to notice, in the briefest way, those last and curious productions of your pen, your six letters to Kirwan. If your papal assumptions and papal logic made your ten letters to "Dear Reader" intolerably dull, you have cast into these so much low personality, so much Episcopal impertinence, and such a strong spice of Irish ill humor, as to make them quite interesting. They are certainly readable productions, and give us new revelations both as to your *fine taste*, and wonderful *good nature*. You cannot expect that I will permit you to raise new issues between you and myself, so as to divert the public mind from the points to which I have solicited its and your attention;—nor can you expect that I could, for a moment, descend to the low level along which in those letters you have seen fit to move. Yet I would respectfully call your attention to a few remarks in reference to them. And this I will do, after the manner of some old preachers, under a few heads.

1. Your letters give us an amusing view of the manner in which you keep your promises. In your first series you say, "I propose to publish a series of letters on the same great topics which Kirwan has discussed." These letters drew "their slow length along," until they reached No. 10, and the "great topics which Kirwan has discussed" were left untouched. Feeling that you could not write such letters upon fish and eggs, you dropped them at the commencement of Lent; they have never since been resumed. In your second series, you say, "Your letters purport to explain the reasons why you left the Roman Catholic Church; . . . the object of mine will be to review those reasons." And yet in your six letters there is not the most remote allusion to "those reasons!" Is this owing, sir, to a want of memory, or to the want of ability? Or is it a sample of the way in which you generally meet your promises? The facts certainly show that you are a most *promising* man.

2. Your letters give us an interesting view of your moral courage. When you commenced your first series we Protestants certainly felt, and said, "Now we are going to have a tract for the times, and worthy of the controversy." But the little spice of the first letter was not found in any other of the series, and they became utterly insipid, and died at the sight of Lent! When the second series commenced, we all said, and the papers, political

and religious, said, "Now we are going to have a racy and manly discussion." Six letters are published without touching a single topic in controversy, and again you retire! And almost before your quill was dry, you were off for Halifax! And when we now inquire after your Right Reverence, the only reply we receive is, "He is gone to Halifax!" If you compare my desertion of the Catholic church when a boy to the desertion of our flag by some of our soldiers in Mexico, to what can we liken your desertion of her in her present exigencies? For a mere stripling recruit to run away in a time of peace, is a small matter; but for the General in Command to flee to Halifax in the very midst of the battle, is a very different affair! I hope you can satisfy "the illustrious Pope Pius IX" as to all this!

3. Your letters furnish a very nice illustration of an easy way of getting out of a difficulty. You expected to make short work of Kirwan's Letters when you commenced answering without reading them. But as you read on, you found the nuts were a little harder to crack than you had anticipated; and you made the commencement of Lent an excuse for dropping them. But this displeased your priests and people, and, as the Freeman's Journal testifies, you were called upon to give to the letters of Kirwan a direct answer. This Papists and Protestants alike desired, and demanded. As there was no way of evasion, in an evil hour

you consented to comply with the demand; and, hence, those six unfortunate letters which have so widely excited a smile at your expense. In these it is obvious that you have read Kirwan. Your temper and your quotations are proof of this. Again you find the nuts too hard to crack; and seeing that instead of crushing them you were covering your own fingers with blood and bruises, you cry out at the close of the sixth letter, "You wish me to dispute with you on matters of general controversy; I must beg leave to decline the proposed honor; I cannot consent to dispute with any man for whom I feel no respect." And after bowing me "for the present, farewell," you are off for Halifax! That is, after laboring through three months of the last winter, and sweltering through six weeks of the present summer, to confute me, in vain, you find out that you have no respect for me, decline further controversy, and flee to Halifax! So that when a man is fairly worsted, he has only to find out that he has no respect for his antagonist, and then he can retire crowned with laurels from the controversy! How easily, according to this rule, could the dastardly Santa Anna have gained a complete victory over the gallant Scott; and even after the Yankees were reveling in the Halls of the Montezumas! He had only to find out that he had no respect for him.

Now, sir, I shrewdly conjecture that this way of getting out of a difficulty is borrowed from "old

Ireland." Did you ever go to school in Ireland; or were those awful laws, of which you speak in your last letter, in force, until after your emigration? Perhaps if you did you may remember that Irish boys are very fond of fighting after school. A very odd scene, which was acted one evening, is now before my mind, as if it transpired but yesterday. There was a large clumsy fellow, that by his boasting and violent gesticulations kept all the boys for some weeks in dread of him; and there was a thin but muscular boy, who at length resolved to meet him in a fair boxing-match. Those of us in the secret retired to a secluded spot and formed a ring; and the fight commenced. It was soon apparent, to the joy of us all, that the thin muscular boy was an overmatch for his opponent. In every round he had signally the advantage. After nearly as many rounds as you have written letters to and about Kirwan, the large clumsy fellow, with his eyes swelled up, and his nose and mouth streaming blood, and scarcely able to stand up, thus addressed the boy that almost pounded him to jelly, "You are a mean, dirty blackguard for whom I have no respect, and I will fight no more with you." Feeling this an additional insult, his antagonist bared his arms for another round, but the beaten boy fled blubbering from the ring; but whither he fled I have no means of knowing. Perhaps your Reverence may find him in Halifax. So you see your way of getting out of a difficulty, although ingenious, is not new. And both you and the public know it is not the true reason.

4. Your letters reveal what may be regarded as a compound estimate of those which I have addressed to you. In your first series you speak of them as "possessing a sprightliness of style which renders them a pleasing contrast to the filthy volumes that have been written on the same side;"—and not long afterwards you speak of them as containing only "clever scurrility." In your six letters, you say of mine, that "so far as regards the grammatical construction of phrases, and a correct and almost elegant use of Anglo-Saxon words, they are not unworthy of the country which produced a Dean Swift, or a Goldsmith." This, from a competent critic would be high praise; and even from you, it shows that your miserably exclusive and debasing religious system has not suppressed all the generous pulsations of your Irish heart. But then you speak of them afterwards as written in the "true wind-bag style." Now, sir, how to reconcile these things, I know not, save on the ground that the "wind-bag" is yours, and that Kirwan's Letters have pricked it, until it has fallen into a state of collapse beyond the power of a new inflation.

5. They reveal a great dishonesty in evading the point of a statement. The Editor of the Observer has already exposed your miserable and truthless perversion of the scene at the Confessional, and, as you well know, drawn by me to the life. The ex-

posure of that single perversion is enough to brand you for life as an unfair man. I say no more about it. So you evade the point of the statement as to the priest reading a dead list from the altar for so much a head per year to pray them out of purgatory. Do you deny that such *a list is read, and that unless the priest is paid he drops the names?* That is the point of the statement. The fact you deny is, a fact not questioned by me, that *any priest ever decides when any soul leaves purgatory!* I have no doubt they will keep souls there as long as they can get money to say mass for them, if it were until St. Tibb's eve, which is the eve after the final consummation.

So you evade the point of the facts as to the drunken priests. You say, and truly, that such facts form no argument against religion, or any form of it; and that you have seen Protestant ministers in state prison for worse sins than drunkenness. But the point of the statement is, that these drunken worthless wretches, whether deposed or recti in ecclesia, *were miracle workers*, and were daily resorted to for miraculous cures both as to men and cattle, and for which they were paid in money and Irish whisky! That, sir, is the point. Have you ever seen a Protestant minister deposed for drunkenness, or in a state prison for a criminal offence, resorted to by Protestants for miraculous cures, and paid for them in money or whisky? If not, where is the point of your parallel? And so as to "St. John's

Well." You say that you "*know nothing about it*," and yet you pronounce the story a fabrication! If you know nothing about it, what right have you to say it is untrue, when millions of living witnesses might be collected in Ireland to the truth of the statement—when the well is there to testify for itself! Sir, is the story about St. Patrick's Well in the County Down a fabrication, whose orgies are a disgrace to the civilized world? Are the Seven Stations at or near Athlone a fabrication, where feats of superstition are yearly performed, which cast into the shade those of the Hindoo fakiers? It is no wonder you are ashamed and vexed when the deep degradation to which popery has reduced our unhappy country, is exposed to the indignant scorn of free and intelligent American citizens;—it is no wonder when you seek, *in any way*, to escape from the obloquy to which the upholding of such a system subjects you.

6. Your letters exhibit a great dislike for the *reductio ad absurdum*. And no wonder, when your system offers so many and such strong temptations to use it. And yet, you know, that it is a legitimate way of reasoning. I hope you cannot say of this, as of St. John's Well, that you know nothing about it. I am striving to show the absurdity of literal interpretation as you use it to prove certain papal tenets; and I ask how, *by your rule*, you escape the inference of being a devil whilst upholding the doctrine of clerical celibacy which Paul

pronounces a doctrine of devils? My object is to show the absurdity of your rule, and yet you seem as vexed about it as if the budding horns had already appeared upon your temples! So as to the text, "he that eateth this bread shall never hunger." The object is to show the unspeakable absurdity of your rule. *If that rule is true*, then all that you have to do is to give your wafer to the poor famishing Irish, and they hunger no more. This you pronounce "a horrible pun on the words of the Saviour;" you mistake,—it is a horrible blow at your ridiculous interpretation of "this is my body." And because the blow is so heavy, it is immediately big with "impiety and inhumanity." Now, sir, the way for you to get rid of all that kind of argument is, to withdraw the premises on which it is built; or when you see that your premises lead to such absurd consequences, to reject them. It will do you no good to get vexed about it.

7. Your letters also exhibit wonderfully cogent proofs of my infidelity. True, all we Protestants are pronounced infidels by you because we are unable "to make an act of faith;" but the proofs of my infidelity are extra, and are furnished by my letters. The first is, I appeal to "common sense" very often. The second is, I eat meat on Friday, and think it neither injures the bodies nor the souls of men. The third is, I believe that intelligent worship is only acceptable to God nor beneficial to me. The fourth is, I do not believe that you can

make God out of a flour wafer. The fifth is, I do not believe that Mary was the mother of God. The sixth is, I do not sufficiently reverence Mary, only speaking of her as "a good woman." The seventh is, I do not highly enough value the lubrication of an old sinner, when dying, with olive oil. The eighth is, I believe it is as acceptable an act to God to worship the head of Balaam's ass, as a human skull said to be that of the Apostle Paul. And all these specifications are melted down and moulded into one great and grand charge, "my insult to the mysteries of the Catholic faith." Well, sir, if these are proofs of my infidelity, I plead guilty. But let me inform you that I draw a distinction between Bible and papal mysteries;—the first I receive as inscrutable and adorable; the second I reject as the mysteries of iniquity. Perhaps my letters are too much pervaded by what you are pleased to call "a silvery thread of wit which is unmistakably Irish," but I have long ago concluded that the scaly hide of the Beast was impervious to reason and argumentation, and that the time has come for Wit and Ridicule and Caricature to empty upon the monster their quiver of arrows. There are some things too absurd to waste reason upon; there is a point beyond which to reason is casting pearls before swine, and where we must answer fools according to their folly. I do not wonder that a mind so *seemingly* superstitious as is yours, should pronounce me occasionally profane; but perhaps you may remember the story of Diodorus about the Roman who inadvertently killed a cat in Egypt, one of the gods of the land. So exasperated were the populace that they ran in frenzy to his house, and neither the files of soldiers drawn up for his protection, nor the terror of the Roman name could save him from being torn to pieces. In times of famine the Egyptians would kill and eat one another before they would kill an ox, a dog, an ibis, or a cat! These were their gods, and to treat them otherwise than with the most profound reverence was unpardonable profanity!!

I accept, sir, most cheerfully, the offer which you make to prove one of my statements, which you question, a fabrication, by a formal investigation, on one condition, which I hope you will have the sense and courage to grant. The condition is this. You say that you do transubstantiate a little wafer into the real and true body and blood of Christ, and that you do this whenever and wherever you say mass. Now "I am willing to go to any reasonable expense to prove this a fabrication, if either you or any other bishop or priest have the courage to meet me in a formal investigation." This will incur but little expense—it can be done at St. Patrick's, or at St. Peter's, or at your own house. You can select three out of the five judges. We will first take the wafer and examine it. You may then say high and low mass over it, and take it through all the required liftings and lowerings needful to transubstantiate it, and if it is not the identical wafer it was when we put it into your hands then we will submit to be branded as blasphemers; but if it is, we will let you off, without any brand, simply as an impostor. The offer which you make would lead to a sea voyage, and would require the raising of the dead, and would lead to some expense; but this can be done in a day, and I will agree to pay the bill.

If you reject this form of the condition, I will make another. Your olive oil, blessed on Maunday Thursday, you represent as possessing wonderful efficacy, when rubbed on a dying sinner according to law. "I am willing to go to any reasonable expense to prove this a fabrication;" and that your olive oil, under these circumstances, has not a whit greater efficacy than whale oil, or bear's oil, or goose grease. And again, I will leave to you the selection of three out of five judges. When these offers are accepted, and these questions are settled, then we will make the required arrangements to meet the challenge which you throw out to myself or Mr. Prime. May I hope to hear from you as soon as it will meet your convenience after your return from Halifax?

In case you should resume this controversy, for the third time, permit me, as your friend, to give you a few words of advice.

1. Keep your temper. A bishop should be no brawler. Good nature is the very air of a good

mind, the sign of a large and generous soul, and the soil in which virtue prospers.

2. Remember that rude assaults upon an opponent do not refute his arguments. You grievously complain of them in your own case; can they be right as to me? If I were all you say of me, and as much beyond that as that is beyond the truth, that would not prove true the absurdities of Romanism—that would not prove that you can create God, and forgive sin,—or that your religion is any thing else but a peacock religion, which has nothing useful or attractive about it save its glittering plumage.

3. Remember that what you write may possibly live after you are dead; and that your office as a bishop gives not the weight of a feather to your weak arguments, whilst it renders your vulgarity doubly vulgar. In this country no man is sustained by his station; unless he graces it, he disgraces himself. The person who raises himself to station, name, and influence, is worthy of double honor; but in case such a person should rise from a cabbage garden to a mitre, he ought to know that the line of conduct which would not particularly dishonor the hoe or the spade, would reflect no enduring reputation upon the crook and the crosier.

Adherence to this advice, if it corrects not your principles, will have, at least, a benign influence on your manners. Farewell. May you be brought to the knowledge of the truth as it is in Jesus.

Yours,

KIRWAN.

LETTER X.

AN APPEAL TO ALL ROMAN CATHOLICS.

My dear Friends,—In closing these letters, as with the two series hitherto published, I turn from Bishop Hughes to you. Many of you have not been uninterested readers of my letters; nor of the controversy, so far as it has assumed that character, between Bishop Hughes and myself. And whilst the prejudices of education, and your respect for official station, would naturally lead you to take sides with him, I am thankful to know that the generous impulses of many of you, and your desire to know the truth, have led you to resolve that I should have fair play. I have appeared before you with no crosses before my name—with no ecclesiastical titles after it—making no flourish of trumpets from the places of brief authority, and with the one simple desire to unfold before your eyes the religious system which has oppressed your fathers, and which in its ceremonial exactions has become too heavy for the earth any longer o bear. And I am thankful that so many, educated as you and I were in our youth, have been led by these letters to seek the religion of Christ and of the Bible among Protestants. And whilst there are many of you whose minds, through priestly interferences, have been so imbued with prejudices as to repel all approach to you, however kind, with the lamp of life and light, yet this is by no means the case with you all. To this latter class, the intelligent and candid of your number, who, in this free land, are determined to think for yourselves, I now appeal.

The history of my "Letters to Bishop Hughes" is a very short one. Whilst yet in my minority, and nearly thirty years ago, I left the Roman Catholic Church. Motives that I now need not detail, led me to write those letters in which I have stated the reasons which induced me to give up the religion of the priest for that of the Bible. To these letters Bishop Hughes attempted an indirect reply in ten letters; and broke down in the midst of the discussion at the commencement of last Lent. As these had nothing in them to answer my objections, or to satisfy your inquiries, you asked for something else. Hence the six letters entitled "Kirwan Unmasked," in which, after abuse without stint or sense, and without answering one solitary objection, he again breaks down at the close of the sixth, and flees to Halifax. And this, my third series, which I now bring to a close, is designed as a reply to those addressed by him to "Dear Reader," and to me, Kirwan.

The history of the Bishop in the concern is about

as short. When my letters first appeared, he could not condescend to answer them! He then commenced answering, without reading them! and without meeting an objection stated by me, he broke down with the tenth letter. When goaded by Catholics and Protestants, until he could stand it no longer, he resolved on a direct answer to my objections; and again he broke down at the close of the sixth letter, without answering one of them. Thinking that it would answer all his purposes with *you* to abuse me, he writes his six wonderful letters, which deserve a place in the museum as a specimen of the controversial taste and ability of popish priests, and again breaks down, and flees beyond seas to hide the shame of his wickedness! How high his calculations on the strength of your prejudices, and on the weakness of your common sense! Having usurped the power of thinking for you, he takes for granted that any kind of episcopal nonsense will satisfy you! But he is mistaken; as multitudes of you declare that his silence would be far better than what he has said, and would have inflicted less injury on Popery in this country.

Such being the history of the letters, look for a moment at the state of the controversy. There, in my first and second series, lie my objections to the Roman Catholic Church, abused from Maine to Mexico, but unanswered. *And I defy Bishop Hughes, and all his mitred brethren on this continent, to answer them on Scriptural and common sense prin-*

ciples, to the satisfaction of any reasonable man. The bishop has published ten letters giving his reasons for adherence to the Roman Catholic Church, out of whose pale there is no salvation. These reasons I have shown to be mere and miserable assumptions, and utterly insufficient to justify the faith or the practice of any living man. Bishop Hughes would not ask your note for a dollar, had he no stronger reasons for asking it than those which he has given to bind you to the Catholic Church; and if he should so impose upon you as to secure your note for no stronger reasons, you might sue him for taking from you your money under false pretences, and send him, if not to purgatory, at least to state prison, to atone for his crime.

Such, then, is the state of this controversy. There lie my objections to popery unanswered. *Let Bishop Hughes answer them, if he can.* There are his reasons for adherence to the Catholic Church confuted. *Let him reconstruct his argument if he can.* And all that he has yet done is, to abuse me in a way unbecoming a bishop, for first riddling his building, and then taking away its foundations. And because the hopes of his gain are gone, he and his priests, were it in their power, would serve me as Paul and Silas were served in Philippi by the masters of the damsel out of whom they cast the spirit of divination. But we are in a free country.

Roman Catholics, from this man and his miserable system, I now turn to you. Read the ten letters which I have reviewed, and see how weak are the arguments for popery! Read the six letters addressed to me, and see how low your bishop can descend! If John Hughes is the Achilles of popery in our country, what must the soldiers under him be!! And will you longer sustain a religion the strong objections to which he cannot meet; and the reasons for adherence to which, as given by himself, are not strong enough to hold up the spider's most attenuated web? Behold him twice coming to the rescue of your church, and twice turning his back without even an effort to spike a single gun aimed at its vitals! Can the system which *he* cannot defend be worthy of *your* support? Can the captain who deserts his post in the heat of battle, be worthy of the commission he bears?

Read his ten letters, if their dullness will permit you, and examine their principles. What an argument for a religious despotism of the most grinding and enduring character! The pope is the successor of Peter, and you have no hope of heaven but in connection with the pope: Be as good, as pious, as charitable, as Godlike as you may, you are out of the way of life unless you submit to the pope, and then to all his subalterns! You have no right to form an opinion of your own; the pope, bishops, and priests are appointed to think for you! Without a license, such as they give in Ireland for selling whisky, you have no right to read the Bible; the priests will do that for you, and tell you what is in it that concerns you! To God your Father you have no right to go save through a priestly intercessor, who, for a fee to suit your circumstances, will transact all your business at the Court of Heaven! All you do you must tell the priest; and thus you give him a power over you by which he can whip you into the traces whenever you dare to think for yourselves! If the letters of Bishop Hughes are true, then the priests of the papal church are a close corporation with the pope at their head, with the keys of life and death in their hands, and through whom alone God exercises spiritual dominion in our world! What a fearful despotism is this, infinitely more oppressive than any civil despotism which has ever cursed the world! It meets you at your entrance into life—it dogs you through every step of your earthly pilgrimage—it stands by you at the bed of death, claiming the power of opening heaven to your soul when it escapes from its clay tabernacle, or of locking it up in hell! From the cradle to the grave you must only do as it ordains at the risk of all the vials of its wrath! And this is popery;—yes, popery as advocated and practised in the city of New-York by Bishop Hughes! With what noble consistency can he raise his voice in Vauxhall against the oppression of Ireland by England, and subscribe his money to buy a shield for the back of the sham-patriots, who, by their shameful blustering and cowardly conduct, have made Irish patriotism a subject of merriment throughout the world;—and then vindicate a code of religious despotism in comparison with which that of Russia is freedom;—and then filch from the pockets of the poor, ignorant, credulous, but noble-hearted and generous Irish, the money they have earned with the sweat of their brow, to purchase for them chains, and to pay priests for riveting them on their limbs! Roman Catholics, will you submit to a despotism which thus degrades, dupes, and robs you? Irish Roman Catholics, so eager to burst the chains with which England has bound the land of our fathers, will you submit to wear a yoke like this? Sons of noble sires, whose blood and bones fatten and whiten every field in Ireland by struggles to break the British yoke, will you, in a land of light and freedom, like Russian serfs, wear a yoke like this? Will you permit a close priestly corporation, without any sufficient motive save to increase their corporate property, to assume over you the power of God—and to bind to their girdle the keys of heaven—to enter your family and to regulate your meat and your drink—if a servant in a Protestant family, to place you there as a spy, and to forbid you enjoying its religious privileges—to think for you—on every hand to surround you with infinitely ramified and potent influences, which are sleepless in their efforts to keep around your neck the yoke of servitude, and to prevent your emancipation into that liberty with which Christ makes his people free? Thousands in this land, and tens of thousands through all the earth, are casting it aside as too heavy longer to be borne; will not all of you do the same? Will you be content to be slaves in a country of freedom,—slaves to papal priests, the most degrading of all slavery—when it is only for you firmly to resolve and you are at once spiritually as you are civilly free? Fling the flag of your spiritual freedom to the free winds of heaven, and let your watchwords be God, the Bible, Liberty, and unborn generations will rise and call you blessed.

Irish Roman Catholics, I am not so destitute of all sympathies with you, and with our fatherland beyond the waves of the Atlantic, as Bishop Hughes would make you believe. I sympathize with you here in that degradation to which the religion of the priest has reduced you. I deeply sympathize with our lovely country at home and our noble countrymen, so deeply degraded, and mainly by the same cause. I renewedly charge upon popery the low social level to which Ireland has been reduced, and the social degradation of her children in all the lands of their dispersion. It is popery that has made her sons and daughters, in so many instances, hewers of wood and drawers of water. And my sympathies with you and for you, more than all other causes, have given existence to these letters. As I early predicted, the bishop rings changes on my apostacy—charges me with desertion—leaves the argument for the man—and in every way, save by reason and argument, seeks to vilify my name, so as to diminish my influence with you. In this he is joined by his priests. But this is simply the conspiracy of the wolves, ravening the fold to induce the sheep to turn a deaf ear to the voice of the shepherd who sounds the alarm. Their craft is in danger, and hence their wrath. I here assert before heaven and earth, that you are grievously imposed upon by your priests—that for the sake of your money they daily practice upon you impositions such as should brand them as impostors—that they traffic in souls, and make a gain of godliness, and that instead of your veneration they are worthy only of your rejection. And for the evidence of all this I need only point you to the moneys which they draw from you by their senseless masses, by their extreme unctions, by their charms, and relics, and penances, and purgatorial deliverances, and by the thousand and one ways in which they show their sympathy for the sheep by fleecing them of their wool. And hence the hue and cry against me by your priests, because I plainly and fearlessly tell you of these things.

Nor am I, Roman Catholics, the profane infidel which your bishop would make me out to be. If there were no alternative for me but to believe what he teaches, I would be again compelled to shoot the gulf of infidelity, and to build my hopes for the future upon the dim twilight instructions of natural religion. What would I not believe sooner than that man can create God! But even were I an infidel, vulgar as Paine, bitter as Voltaire, plausible as Gibbon, would that be any reason why my objections to popery should not be answered? Did not Porteus answer Paine? Did not Campbell confute Hume? And even if an infidel, why should not Bishop Hughes answer my objections? The reason is not in my infidelity, but in his inability. He is unable to answer them. But I am not an infidel. I believe in the Bible. I believe in the religion of Jesus Christ. It is the source of my comforts here, and the foundation of all my hopes for the future. I believe in the divinity, the vicarious atonement of Jesus Christ; and in the efficacy of that atonement to save all, *without money and without price*, who rest solely upon it. "He that believeth in the Lord Jesus Christ," if there was not a pope or priest upon earth, "shall be saved." This is my faith; and it is to this simple, efficacious faith—the faith of the prophets, apostles, martyrs, fathers, confessors of all ages and of all countries—of the true Catholic church in all its ministers and members, that, in my soul, I desire to win you.

Truth, and not mitres, crosses, unmeaning ceremonies, priestly vestments, solemn farces, is the only thing worthy of your love and reverence. Buy the truth and sell it not. Dig for it as for hid treasures. This is the pearl of great price; and, if necessary, sell all that you possess to purchase it. Popery is the religion of children, of low civilization—Christianity is the religion of men, and of high civilization, where the virtues and graces most flourish. Dare to be Christians. Your attachment to popery only benefits the priest; Christianity will enrich yourselves. Dare to be Christians. The night is far spent; the day is at hand. O be children of the day. Fear God, and then the wrath of the priest inspires no more terror than do the gentle whisperings of the evening zephyr.

Praying with all prayer for your deliverance from the degrading and grinding despotism of popery, and for your full emancipation into the glorious liberty of the gospel, I am, with all the sympathies of my Irish nature,

Yours,

KIRWAN.

www.ingramcontent.com/pod-product-compliance
Lightning Source LLC
LaVergne TN
LVHW020233110826
845151LV00003B/912